Learn Microsoft Works in a Day

Jerry Funk

Wordware Publishing, Inc.

Library of Congress Cataloging-in-Publication Data

Funk, Jerry, 1939-
    Learn Microsoft "Works" in a day / by Jerry Funk.
        p.   cm.
    Includes index.
    ISBN 1-55622-205-X
    1. Macintosh (Computer)--Programming.   2. Microsoft Works
    (Computer program).   I. Title.
    QA76.8.M3F86   1991
    005.265--dc20
                                                        90-28607
                                                        CIP

ISBN 1-55622-205-X

10 9 8 7 6 5 4 3 2

9104

All inquiries for volume purchases of this book should be addressed to Wordware
Publishing, Inc., at the above address. Telephone inquiries may be made by calling:

(214) 423-0090

Contents

CHAPTER 3 — SPREADSHEET

CHAPTER 4 — DATABASE

Chapter 1

INTRODUCTION

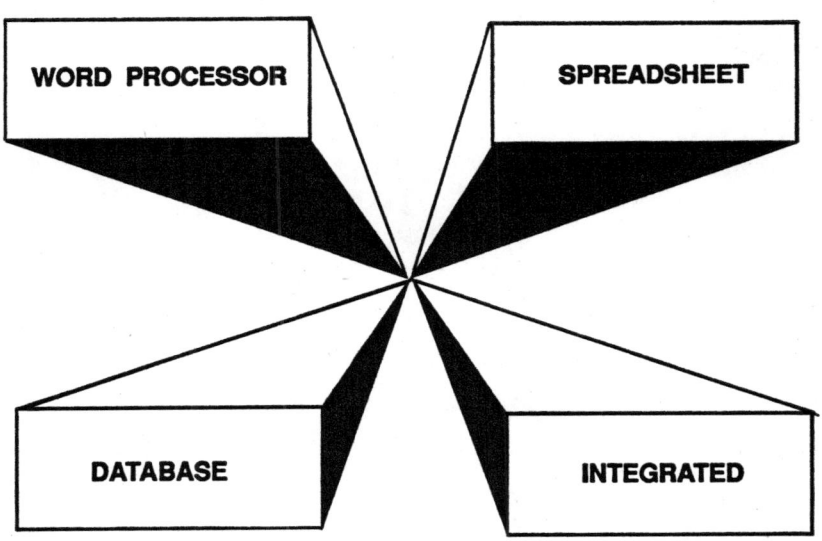

Microsoft WORKS is known as an integrated software package. When software is integrated, that usually means your files can easily be shared between computer program applications that are normally designed for a specific purpose.

There are many fine word processor software programs, spreadsheet programs, and database programs available, but they usually work independently. Many times your output (files) cannot easily be shared by one of the other types of software programs. Microsoft WORKS is designed to provide you with an easy way to share your files between these kinds of application programs.

Integrated also means that the menu commands and procedures are similar for each of the applications. As an example, this means you can use the same menu and menu commands to print a file from the word processor that you use from the spreadsheet or the database. Some of those integrated procedures that are most commonly used in WORKS will be introduced in this chapter. When you learn them for one program, you can do the same thing for the other programs.

OVERVIEW

The Microsoft WORKS software package has FOUR major computer applications:

The Word Processor—designed to write letters, research papers, memos, etc. and to effectively replace the typewriter. It enables you to easily make corrections, move text, add text, and make many other revisions with a minimum of effort.

The Spreadsheet—intended mainly for manipulating numbers and using formulas. The data can easily be sorted in a different order and you can quickly test an unending series of "what if" situations.

The Database—serves as a computerized filing system. It can sort entries, copy, move, change, find, and organize the data alphabetically or numerically.

Communications—allows computer information to be sent over the phone lines. It is used for such things as mail delivery and for communicating with an increasing number of information services that offer electronic bulletin boards, up-to-date stock market quotes, news and sports information, airline reservations, and even computer shopping.

TERMINOLOGY

Files, documents, and disks   When you write a letter with the word processor or create a spreadsheet or a database, the information shown on the computer screen is only temporarily available as an electronic image. When you turn off the computer, the electronic data is lost unless it has first been stored on some physical device. Some computers have a built-in *disk* (hard drive) to store it on permanently in addition to the (5.25" or 3.5") *floppy disks* that can be carried from one computer to another. The data is called a *file* (or document) and the procedure of storing it permanently to a disk is called *saving* the file to disk. These files can then be retrieved (opened) for further editing at a later time.

File names   When a computer stores a file permanently to a disk, the file must have a name so the computer can distinguish it from other files. This name may consist of not more than eight characters. Characters are combinations of letters and numbers and special symbols like these: # ! % @ − ( ). BLANK SPACES ARE NOT ALLOWED IN A FILE NAME.

Legal File Names	*Illegal File Names*
Letter-1	Report 1 (space in it)
Budget	AprilBudget (too long)

File extension   A file name is "extended" by using a period (.) and three additional characters. For this software package, it is best to allow the computer to automatically attach the extension. It will attach one of the following:

.WPS	for a Word Processor file
.WKS	for a Spreadsheet file
.WDB	for a Database file
.WCM	for a Communications file

The directory The directory lists all of the file names you have on your disk. In WORKS the directory is accessed by the File Menu and it divides the files into four sections: Word Processor, Spreadsheet, Database, and Other Files (the files are alphabetized within each section).

The Window Menu and the active file WORKS allows you to open and have ready for use up to eight files at one time. These files are all listed and numbered for you in the bottom portion of the Window Menu. The file that is currently showing on the computer screen is called the *active file*. Using the Window Menu and selecting a different file (by number or by using the selection bar) will exchange the active file with the one you selected from the Window Menu.

HOW TO OPEN FILES AND SAVE FILES

To open or to save a file, you must use the File Menu. It looks like this:

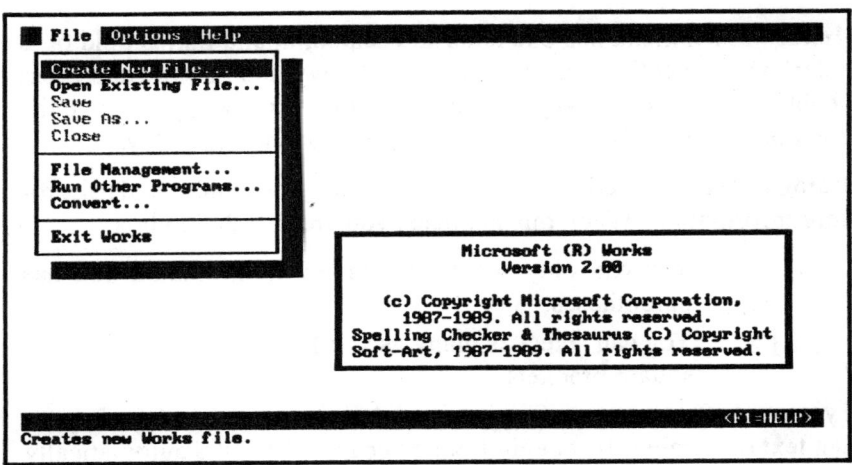

Create New File Selecting the first option from the File Menu brings up another options box (see following) that allows you to access any one of the four types of software applications available.

Open Existing File   Selecting this command from the File Menu will activate a screen that shows what is available. Using the Down Arrow key to move the selection bar over the file you want and pressing Enter opens that file. When a file is opened, only a duplicate copy is loaded to the computer's memory. The original file is not changed on the disk until you save the changes.

Save a file   The name of the file is shown just below the menu line on the title bar. When it is first created, WORKS gives it a file name that is used until you change it. There are two types of saving:

1. The Save command overwrites your original file and uses the *same* name.

2. The Save As command saves your work to a new file under a *different* name and leaves the original file unchanged on the disk.

MENUS AND DIALOG BOXES

Menus   Each menu has one letter in each command that is bold or is underlined. To activate a command, hold down the Alt key and press the letter. An alternate way is to use the Down Arrow key to move the selection bar over the command and then press the Enter key.

Dialog boxes   Sometimes a command offers you choices and asks for more information. When this happens, you are in a dialog box.

( )   You can only select *one* choice if the dialog box has parentheses.

[ ]   You can select as many as you like if the dialog box has square brackets.

If you see text or numbers within square brackets, you can type in your own text or number. Just begin typing because WORKS automatically deletes the text for you when you start typing.

The Alt key   To be able to access the commands available in the menus, you first must press the Alt key. When you do this, you allow menus and commands to be selected just by pressing the highlighted letter.

The Esc key   The Esc key allows you to "escape" back to what you were doing without any action being taken.

Insert mode This means that wherever the cursor is, the next character typed will be in that spot on the screen and all previous text will be moved over to the right to make room for that character. If you want that character to *replace* a character, you have to delete the character to be replaced because it does not type over it when in the insert mode. When using the word processor, you are automatically in the insert mode.

USING A MOUSE

If your system has a mouse, there will be an arrow on the screen if you are in graphics mode or a small rectangle if you are in text mode. This mouse "pointer" can be moved around the screen by moving the mouse on the desktop.

The mouse has two or more buttons that can be pressed (clicked) to initiate an action you want. One click is used to make a choice. Two clicks in rapid succession (double click) is used in place of pressing the Enter key.

The mouse is particularly useful when making menu choices and in moving the cursor directly to a word or character in your file on the screen. To do this, move the cursor to any character and click the left mouse button. The cursor will now appear directly under the character you moved to. After a menu and its option is chosen, some of the other choices that you can make with the mouse are:

Move the mouse pointer inside a *text box* and click the left mouse button. Then type in the information needed.

In a *list box*, click the down scroll arrow to see all choices available. Then double click on the option you want.

In a *check box*, click on the choice you want and an "X" will appear between the parentheses.

For a *command button*, point at the action you want to take and click to carry out that action.

Select a character:

1. Point to the character
2. Click the *left* mouse button

Select a word:

1. Point to the word
2. Click the *right* mouse button

Select a sentence:

1. Point anywhere in the sentence
2. Click *both* mouse buttons at the same time

Select a line:

1. Point in the margin to the left of the line
2. Click the *left* mouse button

Select a paragraph:

1. Point in the margin to the left of the paragraph
2. Click the *right* mouse button

Select the entire document:

1. Point anywhere in the left margin
2. Click *both* mouse buttons at the same time

Chapter 2

WORD PROCESSOR

The word processor is designed to write letters, research papers, memos, etc. and to very effectively replace the typewriter. It enables you to easily make corrections, move text, add text, and make many other revisions with a minimum of effort.

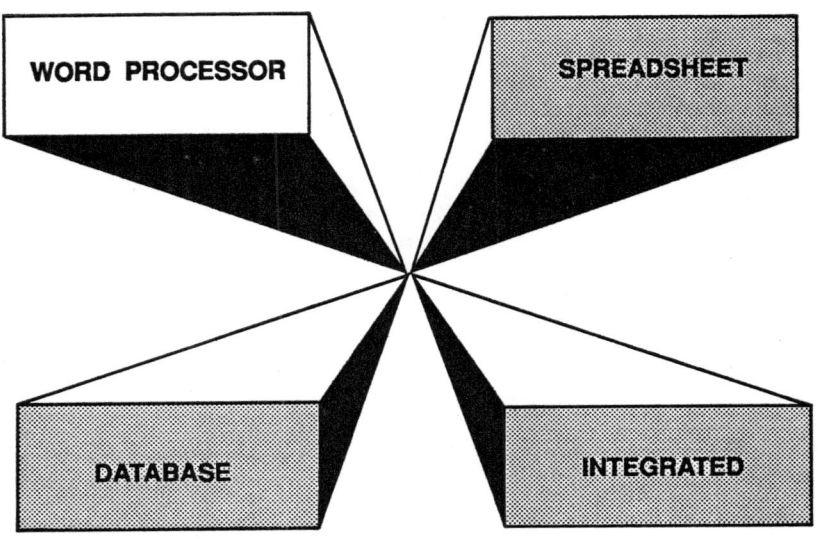

SECTION 1

Skills to be learned in this section

- Starting a new file
- Opening an existing file
- Learning the screen characters
- Inserting a blank line
- Using the Save As command
- Printing a file

STARTING A NEW FILE

A new file is one that has not yet been created and is not on the disk.

Do this:

1. Select **Create New File** from the File Menu **[F/N]**.

2. In the program selection dialog box, just press **Enter** to choose "New Word Processor."

3. The word processor opens a work area for you with the word processor menu on the top line and a temporary file name, "WORD1.WPS," on the second line.

4. Press **Alt-F-C** to close the file with no entries made in it.

OPENING AN EXISTING FILE

An existing file is one that is already stored on a disk. You need to know the file name before it can be opened. Once it is opened, it is included in the bottom of the Window Menu in the list of files that are open.

Do this:

1. Select **Open Existing File** from the File Menu **[F/O]**.

2. In the "File to open" dialog box, press **Down Arrow** once to move the cursor to the "Files:" box.

3. Continue to press **Down Arrow** until the highlighted selection bar covers this file: DRILL-1.WPS and press **Enter**.

4. That file will be the "active file" until you open a new file. Press **Alt-W** and you see the file DRILL-1.WPS in the Window Menu as a numbered file that is currently open.

5. Press the **Esc** key.

LEARNING THE SCREEN CHARACTERS

There are several characters that the word processor uses to visually show you where spaces and tabs are, end of paragraphs, etc. These characters can be seen or hidden using the Options Menu and the Show All Characters command.

Do this:

1. If you have not already done so, open the file DRILL-1.WPS.

2. Make sure the spacing characters are showing on the screen (you will see a small down arrow between the first two paragraphs). If the characters are not showing, use the Options Menu and select the **Show All Characters** command.

3. Read through the DRILL-1 file to learn about these special screen characters.

INSERTING A BLANK LINE

A blank line can be inserted two ways. It will cause the cursor to be advanced to the left margin and down one line.

Do this:

1. While still in the DRILL-1 file, press **Enter**, or

2. Hold down **Shift** and press **Enter** (press Shift + Enter).

USING THE SAVE AS COMMAND

This command renames an existing file already on the disk or changes the temporary file name assigned by WORKS if it is a new file.

Do this:

1. With DRILL-1.WPS still the active file, select **Save As** from the File Menu **[F/A]**.

2. Between the "Save file as:" brackets type **DRILL-1A** as the new file name (just start typing, the old name will be erased as soon as you start).

3. Press **Enter**.

4. Select **Open Existing File** from the File Menu **[F/O]**.

5. Move the cursor with the Down Arrow through the "Files" box and notice now that there are two separate files that are identical, but with different names (DRILL-1.WPS and DRILL-1A.WPS).

6. Press **Esc** to return to DRILL-1A.WPS and then close it **(Alt-F-C)**.

PRINTING A FILE

To be able to get a hard copy (a paper printout) of your files, you must have a printer hooked up and set for this software.

Do this:

1. Open the DRILL-1.WPS file to make it an active file.

2. Select **Print** from the Print Menu **[P/P]**.

3. In the "Number of copies:" dialog box, just press **Enter** (this should cause the two-page file to be printed).

4. Compare your printout with the key on the next page.

5. Close this file now, **Alt-F-C.**

KEY: DRILL-1.WPS
Chapter 2 - Section 1

The character immediately after the title and immediately following this sentence is what WORKS uses for the paragraph symbol.

The down arrow symbol between these first two paragraphs shows an end-of-line, but not the end of a paragraph. It is made by holding the **Shift** key down while pressing the **Enter** key **Shift + Enter**.

In these paragraphs, the small dot between words, but not at the bottom of the line, shows where spaces are.

   The right arrow at the beginning of this sentence shows that a "tab" has been used.

Note: The text *content* above is relevant only when it appears on the computer screen.

The dotted line above, coupled with the ">>" markers at the left of this sentence, shows where the first line of a "new page" will be. It is created by pressing **Shift + Enter**. The ">>" markers in the left margin without the dotted line across the screen shows where the first line of a new page is when WORKS automatically sets it, <u>not</u> when you force it.

The "diamond" symbol at the bottom left corner of the work area identifies the end of the entire file.

Note: The text *content* above is relevant only when it appears on the computer screen.

DRILL-2

Tasks   This drill lets you practice the following:

- Starting a new file
- Typing in text
- Entering a blank line
- Renaming and saving a file
- Printing a file

Procedure   From the information below, complete the steps for DRILL-2.

If you have any problems, review the material in Chapter 2, Section 1.

1. Open a new word processor file. The program automatically gives it the name WORD1.WPS.

2. Starting in the upper left corner of the work area where the cursor is blinking, type the following paragraph. Correct any errors as you type. Do *not* press the Enter key unless instructed to. This allows your lines to wrap automatically.

    The objective in this drill is to familiarize you with some features of the word processor. As you type, you will notice that any word near the right margin that cannot be finished on that same line will be moved to the next line.

3. Press the **Enter** key after the period in that paragraph.

4. Hold down the **Shift** key and press the **Enter** key again. If the special characters are not showing on your screen, use the Options/Show All Characters commands. Notice that the Shift + Enter keys caused a line feed but not an end of paragraph marker.

5. Now type this last sentence.

    This feature is called "word wrap," which means you do not have to worry about a carriage return like you do with a typewriter.

6. Select **File/Save As** and rename the file DRILL-2.WPS.

7. Select **Print/Print** and get a printout of your file.

8. Compare your printout with the key on the following page.

KEY: DRILL-2.WPS
Chapter 2 - Section 1

The objective in this drill is to familiarize you with some features of the word processor. As you type, you will notice that any word near the right margin that cannot be finished on that same line will be moved to the next line.

This feature is called "word wrap," which means you do not have to worry about a carriage return like you do with a typewriter.

SECTION 2

Skills to be learned in this section

- Selecting text
- Moving text
- Deleting text
- Copying text
- Centering text

SELECTING TEXT

Whether using the word processor, the spreadsheet, or the database, there is a need to select text or numbers for editing purposes. When you want to copy, move, delete, bold, italicize, or underline *after* it is typed, the text needs to first be selected so the program recognizes which text should be edited.

To make a selection, you position the cursor on the first character where the editing will begin. Then you press the F8 key. This action will cause *EXT* to be displayed on the bottom right portion of your screen (indicating you should now "extend," or move, the cursor to the last character where the editing will end). As you "extend" the cursor, the text is highlighted so you can visually see what was selected. At this point you need to take whatever action is appropriate (move the text, delete the text, etc.).

Note: If your selection continues all the way to the end of your document, after you press the F8 key you can then press the Ctrl-End keys together and the remainder of the document is selected.

Do this:

1. Open a new word processor file and type the following:

   The word BOLD will be formatted as bold print.

2. Move the cursor to the "B" in BOLD and press **F8** to turn on the selection.

3. Press **Right Arrow** until the highlighting covers the "D" in BOLD.

4. Press **Alt, t, B** in that order and the word "BOLD" is now in bold print.

5. Close the file without saving it.

MOVING TEXT

Moving text is transferring it to a different place in that same file. Text *cannot* be moved to another file, just copied. Before it can be moved, it must first be selected using the F8 key. After it is moved, it is no longer in its original location.

Do this:

1. Open the file DRILL-3.WPS from your data disk.

2. Notice that "Sentence #2" is not between #1 and #3. Move the cursor to the "S" in "Sentence #2" and press **F8**.

3. Press **Right Arrow** until the entire paragraph is highlighted.

4. Select **Move** from the Edit Menu.

5. Move the cursor to one of the paragraph markers between sentence #1 and sentence #3 and press **Enter**. The text you selected should have been moved.

6. Save the changed file using the **File/Save** command.

7. Close the file.

DELETING TEXT

Deleting text removes it from your file completely. Deleting can be accomplished a character at a time by using the Del key. When a block of text is to be deleted, it is more efficient to first select it using the F8 key.

Do this:

1. Open the DRILL-3.WPS file from your data disk.

2. Locate the sentence that says it should be deleted.

3. Select the entire sentence using the **F8** key.

4. Choose **Delete** in the Edit Menu. The sentence should have been deleted. (**Note:** Instead of accessing the Edit Menu, you could have just pressed the Del key.)

5. Save the changed file using the **File/Save** command.

6. Close the file.

COPYING TEXT

The copy feature is almost identical to the move feature, except when text is copied it is then located in more than one place. Text can be copied between files but text cannot be moved between files.

Do this:

1. Open the file DRILL-3.WPS from your data disk and notice the line of dashes just above "Sentence #1." You are going to *copy* that line.

2. Move the cursor to the first dash at the extreme left margin and press **F8** twice to select that entire line.

3. Choose **Copy** from the Edit Menu.

4. Move the cursor somewhere *below* all of the text and press **Enter** (there should now be two lines of dashes).

CENTERING TEXT

To center text, you can use the Center command in the Format Menu or the shortcut Ctrl-C keys. This will cause the text in that paragraph to be centered, regardless of the margin settings. Centering is released by using the Normal Paragraph command in the Format Menu or more quickly with the Ctrl-X keys.

You can activate centering prior to typing text (press Ctrl-C) and as you type text, it will be centered.

Do this:

1. With the DRILL-3 file still open, place the cursor somewhere in this line:

   Selecting and the F8 Key

2. Press **Ctrl-C** (this should have caused the text to be centered).

3. With the cursor still located on that line, press **Ctrl-X** and the centering is released.

4. Center that sentence again and save it using **Save** from the File Menu.

5. Get a printout (**Alt-P-P**).

6. Compare your printout to the key on the following page. Drill-3 should look like the following after all of the changes are made.

```
╔══════════════════════════════════════════════════╗
║ ┌────────────────────────────────────────────────┐ ║
║ │              KEY: DRILL-3.WPS                  │ ║
║ │            Chapter 2 - Section 2               │ ║
║ └────────────────────────────────────────────────┘ ║
```

Selecting and the **F8** key

Sentence #1: Text must first be selected for editing, copying, moving or deleting. The character, word, sentence or block of text must be highlighted using the **F8** key.

Sentence #2: Once the text has been selected, the program then needs to know what action should be taken. Most often this next step accesses the Edit Menu.

Sentence #3: The Move, Copy and Delete commands are found in the Edit Menu.

SECTION 3

Skills to be learned in this section

- Setting tab stops
- Setting margins
- Justifying text
- Changing line spacing
- Creating hanging paragraphs
- Creating headers and footers

SETTING TAB STOPS

You set, clear, or change tab stops by choosing the Tabs command from the Format Menu. In WORKS, tab stops are preset at one-half-inch intervals starting from the left margin. When you set a tab stop, all default tab stops to the left of your tab stop are cleared. The settings affect only the current paragraph. Your tab stops appear as letters on the ruler line. The letter on the ruler line indicates the position and alignment you have chosen.

L = aligns *left* edge of text at the tab stop.

C = *centers* text at the tab stop.

R = aligns *right* edge of text at the tab stop.

D = lines the *decimal point* in a number with the tab stop. If the text has no decimal point, then it aligns the left edge of text at the tab stop.

Steps to Set a Tab Stop

1. From the Format Menu, choose the Tabs command.

2. In the "Position" text bracket, type the tab stop number.

3. In the "Alignment" box, select left, right, center, or decimal.

4. In the "Leader" box select the leader you want (none, dots, dashes, underline, or equal signs).

5. Press Alt+I for Insert to register your selection.

6. Repeat steps 2 through 5 above for *each* tab you want.

7. When you have all tab stops set, press Alt+D for Done to exit.

Note: You will need to set tab stops one at a time for each column you need.

SETTING MARGINS

The default margins are set 1.3 inches from the left side of the page and 1.2 inches from the right side. You will be able to see the left margin symbol ([) and the right margin symbol (]) on the ruler line at the top of the screen. The default distance for margins at the top and bottom of the page is 1 inch. The margins can be changed by using the Page Setup & Margins command in the Print Menu.

Page Setup & Margins Dialog Box

```
 Top margin:     [1"......]  Page length:    [11".....]
 Bottom margin:  [1"......]  Page width:     [8.5"....]
 Left margin:    [1.3"....]
 Right margin:   [1.2"....]  1st page number: [1....]
 Header margin:  [0.5"....]
 Footer margin:  [0.5"....]

                             <  OK  >  <Cancel>
```

Do this:

1. Open a new word processing file by selecting "New Word Processor" [F/N].

2. Select **Tabs** from the Format Menu.

3. Type **1.5** in the "Position" brackets and press **Alt+I** for "Insert."

4. Type **4.2** in the "Position" brackets.

5. Move the cursor to the "Alignment" box and type **C** to activate center alignment.

6. Press **Alt+I** for "Insert" and then **Alt+D** for "Done" to exit the tabs dialog box and return you to your work area in the word processor file.

7. Press **Tab** and then type **left tab stop**.

8. Press **Tab** again and type **center tab stop**.

9. Press **Enter** and leave the file open for the next drill.

The line you typed and the ruler line should now look like this:

```
[··········1···L····2·········3·········4·C·······5·········]
→              left·tab·stop→     center·tab·stop¶
¶
◆
```

Notice the text alignment in relation to the tab stop on the ruler line.

JUSTIFYING TEXT

When you want your text to be lined up evenly at the right margin too, you justify it. You can select justification from the Format Menu, but it is easier to set it and remove it with the Ctrl-J (to set it) and the Ctrl-X (to remove it) shortcut keystrokes.

Do this:

1. In the open file, press **Ctrl-J** and then type the following paragraph:

   Justification can be set before typing begins or it can be set after the text is already typed. As long as the cursor is anywhere inside the paragraph, that entire paragraph can be set or released at one time.

2. Make sure the cursor is somewhere inside the paragraph you just typed and press **Ctrl-X** (and watch the right margin justification be released).

3. Close the file without saving it.

Note: As long as the cursor is anywhere inside the paragraph, Ctrl-J and Ctrl-X will alternately justify and release justification.

CHANGING LINE SPACING

The technique used for setting the spacing between lines of text is similar to that used for justification of text. The Ctrl-X keystrokes release any special line spacing after it has been set and the shortcut keystrokes that follow set it.

For *single spaced* paragraphs press **Ctrl+1**.
For *double spaced* paragraphs press **Ctrl+2**.
For *1 1/2 spaced* paragraphs press **Ctrl+5**.

CREATING HANGING PARAGRAPHS

To indent the entire paragraph use the Ctrl-H shortcut keystrokes. This causes the left margin of the paragraph to be aligned at the tab stop for the paragraph. You can "unhang" a paragraph by pressing Ctrl-G while the cursor is anywhere inside the paragraph.

CREATING HEADERS AND FOOTERS

A *header* is text that can be repeated at the *top* of every page in a document. A *footer* is the same as a header, but it appears at the *bottom* of the page. In WORKS software, you can have "standard" or "paragraph" headers and footers, but *not* both types at the same time. The examples in this book are confined to standard headers and footers.

The standard headers and footers are automatically centered unless you use codes that can cause them to be printed at the left or right margins. The standard header or footer is useful for quick and easy preset text that does not exceed one line.

Standard Headers and Footers

1. Choose Headers & Footers from the Print Menu.
2. Go to the "Headers" text box and type text and/or codes.
3. Go to the "Footers" text box and type text and/or codes.

Note: If you do *not* want a header on the first page, move to the appropriate box that says, "No header on 1st page," and turn it on. You can do the same for a footer. The codes that were mentioned above are provided in the MEMDRILL at the end of this section.

TABDRILL

Tasks   This drill lets you practice the following:

- Set tab stops
- Select tab "leaders"

Procedure   From the information below, complete the steps for TABDRILL.

If you have any problems, review the material in Chapter 2, Section 3.

1. Open the file TABDRILL.WPS from your data disk.

2. Starting two lines below the ruler line on the screen, set the following tabs using the Tab command in the Format Menu:

   a. Set a **left** tab stop at 1" with no leader.
   b. Set a **right** tab stop at 3" with leader #3 (underline).
   c. Set a **center** tab stop at 5" with leader #3 (underline).
   d. Set a **decimal** tab stop at 6" with leader #3 (underline).

3. Tab to each tab stop and type the following information. Be sure to press **Shift+Enter** at the end of each line and not just Enter.

Jones	Bill	Texas	5.32
Archer	Ann	Maine	126.15
Smith	Herb	Florida	45.99
Benson	William	Colorado	.75

4. Use **Save** from the File Menu and save it to your disk.

5. Use **Print** from the Print Menu and print it.

6. Position the cursor on "Florida." Actually, anywhere within that paragraph is fine since you used the Shift+Enter for down linefeeds. This means any changes in the tab settings will be applied to all lines in that paragraph at one time. Go to the tab menu and type **3** in the "Position" box and then press **Alt-L** and **Alt-N** and then **Enter** to change the second tab stop and the leader. Press **Alt-D** to escape and notice the difference.

7. Don't save these latest changes, just close the file and answer "no."

8. Compare your printout to the key on the following page.

```
╔══════════════════════════════════════════════════╗
║ ┌────────────────────────────────────────────────┐ ║
║ │              KEY: TABDRILL                      │ ║
║ │           Chapter 2 - Section 3                 │ ║
║ └────────────────────────────────────────────────┘ ║
╚══════════════════════════════════════════════════╝

[.........L.........2........_R.........4........_C.........D...]

        Jones_____Bill_____Texas_____5.32
        Archer_____Ann_____Maine____126.15
        Smith_____Herb_____Florida____45.99
        Benson_____William_____Colorado_____.75
```

MEMDRILL

Tasks This drill lets you practice the following:

- Justify text
- Create hanging paragraphs
- Change line spacing
- Reset margins
- Create headers and footers

Procedure From the information below, complete the steps for MEMDRILL.

If you have any problems, review the material in Chapter 2, Section 3.

1. Open the file MEMDRILL.WPS from your data disk.

2. Choose **Page Setup & Margins** from the Print Menu.

    a. Move to the "Left margin" brackets and type **1**.
    b. Move to the "Right margin" brackets and type **1**.
    c. Press **Enter** to leave the dialog box.

3. Put the cursor inside the first paragraph.

    a. Press **Ctrl-J** to justify that paragraph.
    b. Press **Ctrl-2** to double space the paragraph.

4. Put the cursor inside each of the next two paragraphs and press **Ctrl-H, Ctrl-J** and **Ctrl-2** to activate the hanging paragraph feature with double spacing and justification.

5. Choose **Headers & Footers** from the Print Menu.

    a. In the "Header" box type **Codes for Standard Headers & Footers**.
    b. Move to the "Footer" box and type **&l Memo Drill &r Page &p**.
    c. Press **Alt-N** to put an "X" in the "No header on 1st page" brackets.
    d. Press **Alt-O** to put an "X" in the "No footer on 1st page" brackets.
    e. Press **Enter** to leave the dialog box.

6. Get a printout and use the **Save** command from the File Menu to save it to your disk, then close the file [**Alt-F-C**].

7. Compare your printout to the key on the following pages.

KEY: MEMDRILL
Chapter 2 - Section 3

MEMO

TO: WORKS User

FROM: The Author

SUBJECT: Header and Footer Codes

   The codes on the next page can be used for standard headers and footers. These codes can be entered in the text boxes along with the text. You can include as many codes as you want in a single header or footer. Without a code, the text will automatically be centered.

[]   The header and footer margins in the Page Setup & Margins dialog box have a default setting of .5 inch. This is the distance from the top or bottom of the page.

[]   The header and footer margin settings have to be smaller than the settings for the top (of the page) margin or the bottom (of the page) margin.

```
            Codes for Standard Headers & Footers


   ---------------------------------------------------------------
                    Header & Footer Codes
   ---------------------------------------------------------------

     If you want to do this                    Type in this

   align any text at the left margin.................. &l

   align any text at the right margin............... &r

   center text between the margins................... &c

   print the page number............................. &p

   print the file name............................... &f

   print the date.................................... &d

   print the time.................................... &t

   print the ampersand (&) character itself.......... &&
   ---------------------------------------------------------------

   Note: You can use the Edit/Insert Special commands to
   insert the date, time, filename, etc. too.

   Example:    &l Quarterly Report    &cp.&p   &r&d

               The header above would look like this
               when printed: (without the border)

   ---------------------------------------------------------------
   Quarterly Report              p.1              3/31/90
   ---------------------------------------------------------------


   Memo Drill                                    Page 2
```

Chapter 3
SPREADSHEET

The spreadsheet is intended mainly for manipulating numbers and using formulas. The data can easily be sorted in many different ways and you can quickly test an unending series of "what if" questions.

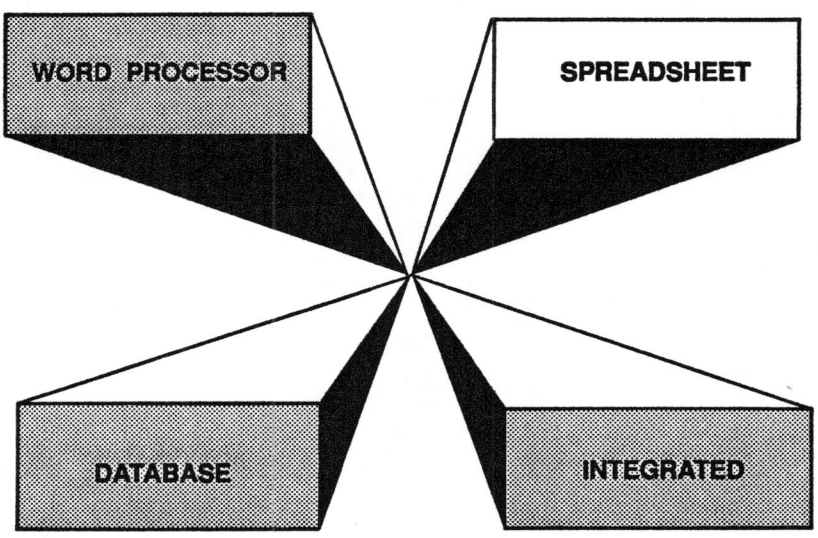

SECTION 1

Skills to be learned in this section

- Cursor movement
- Cells and ranges
- Numbers, formulas, and text
- Selecting a range
- Printing procedures
- Editing entries
- Clearing (erasing) cell contents
- Deleting rows and columns
- Inserting rows and columns

CURSOR MOVEMENT

The arrow keys move you one cell at a time. The Home key returns you to column A on the row you are on. Ctrl + Home will return you to cell A1. Ctrl + End takes you to the last row in the spreadsheet. The End key takes you to the last cell in the spreadsheet that has something in it on that row. Pressing F5 and specifying a cell address allows you to move immediately to that location.

CELLS AND RANGES

A spreadsheet is made up of columns and rows. Each column has a lettered heading ("A," "E," etc.) and each row has a numbered heading ("1," "8," etc.).

Each column and row intersects to form a _cell._ Column B and row 3 intersect to form cell B3. B3 is called a _cell reference._ The information you store in your spreadsheet is stored in cells.

A rectangular group of cells is called a _range._ Ranges can be as small as one cell or as large as the entire spreadsheet. Many of the commands, such as Copy or Move, work for ranges as well as for cells.

A range reference determines which cells are in a range. The *range reference* is the cell reference for the upper left corner of the range and the lower right corner, separated by a colon. (Example: A1:B4)

The *formula bar* shows the contents of the active cell, which is the highlighted cell you are working with. The formula bar is where you enter and edit text, numbers, and formulas. Pressing Enter places what is in the formula bar into the active cell.

To make another cell the active cell, use the direction keys. The new active cell's contents then are displayed in the menu bar.

NUMBERS

Numbers express a quantity. They can be integers (25), decimal numbers (5.8), or fractions (5 4/5). Numbers can be entered with commas, decimals, minus signs, parentheses, fraction bars, percent signs, and dollar signs.

Examples:　　　2234　　2,234　223.4　　−223
　　　　　　　(223)　10 3/4　2%　　$12.50

When you enter a number that contains a dollar sign ($) before the number or a percent sign (%) after the number, WORKS automatically formats the cell for a dollar amount or for a percentage amount. A number in parentheses is interpreted as a *negative number*.

Note: If the formatted number you enter is too long to display within the width of the cell, WORKS displays '######' in the cell. If you widen the column enough, then the number will be displayed in the cell's format.

FORMULAS

A formula is an equation that is used to calculate a value. When you enter formulas, you type an equal sign first. Formulas can contain numbers, cells, range references, arithmetic operators (like "+" and "−"), and functions (like SUM, SQRT).

A function, such as SUM, is a built-in equation you can use to solve a complicated calculation. WORKS has 57 built-in functions.

TEXT

Text is anything that is not a number or a formula. To display numbers as text instead of numbers, precede them with a quotation mark (").

SELECTING A RANGE

A range with a single cell is selected just by putting the cursor in that cell. To select a multiple cell range, move the cursor to the top left cell of the range and press F8. This holds one corner of the selection in place while the range is extended by using the arrow keys to move to the cell in the bottom right corner of the range. Selection is necessary when you want to format, move, or copy cells in the range all at one time.

Do This:

1. In a blank spreadsheet type **1** in cell A1, **2** in cell B1 and **3** in cell C1.

2. Move the cursor back to cell A1 and press **F8.**

3. Move the cursor to cell C1 and press **Enter.**

Note: Notice the range A1:C1 that you selected is now highlighted. You could now collectively format, move, or copy the cells in the selected range. Pressing Esc twice deselects a previously selected range when that range is still highlighted.

PRINTING PROCEDURES

The printing procedures are the same for a spreadsheet as for the word processor. To print just a portion of the spreadsheet and not the rest, you have to select the range to print and use the Set Print Area command in the Print Menu.

EDITING ENTRIES

Editing means making changes to numbers, formulas, or text you have already entered into a cell. You edit one cell at a time. Pressing F2 puts you in the edit mode in the formula bar. The status line displays EDIT when you are in the edit mode. You can retype the characters to be edited or change them one character at a time.

CLEARING (ERASING) CELL CONTENTS

The Clear command in the Edit Menu erases the contents of the selection you made. The cell and its format remain in the spreadsheet. If cell A1 contains the number 10 in dollar format, clearing the cell removes the number 10 but leaves the cell with dollar format. Any new number or formula typed into the cell would be displayed in dollar format. Deleting, on the other hand, removes the entire row or column of cells from the spreadsheet, leaving nothing behind. **Note:** To clear a *single* cell, press Backspace and then Enter.

DELETING ROWS AND COLUMNS

The Delete Row/Column command from the Edit Menu or the Del key removes selected columns or rows from the spreadsheet. To delete a row or a column, select it by using the F8 key and the arrow keys and then press the Del key. **Deleted information cannot be recovered, so be careful.** Also, you must be careful not to delete cells that other formulas refer to. If you do, WORKS replaces the references to the deleted cells with the error value ERR.

INSERTING ROWS AND COLUMNS

The Insert Row/Column command from the Edit Menu lets you add as many rows or columns as you want. When a row is inserted, it appears on the row where the cell pointer (cursor) is located and all rows on or below the cell pointer are moved down. When a column is inserted, all columns on or to the right of the cell pointer are moved to the right to make room for the new column.

Do this:

1. Open a new spreadsheet.
2. Type the 12 labels in the cells as shown below.

	A	B	C	D
1	A1	B1	C1	D1
2	A2	B2	C2	D2
3	A3	B3	C3	D3
4	A4	B4	C4	D4

3. Press **F5** (Go To key), type **D3**, and press **Enter**. The cursor should have moved immediately to cell location D3.
4. Press **Home** and the cursor moves to the column A cell (A3) in that row.
5. Press **Ctrl + Home** to move to cell A1.
6. Press **End** to move to the last cell on that row (D1).
7. Press **Ctrl + End** to move to the last cell in the spreadsheet that has something in it (D4).
8. Move the cursor to C2.

   a. Choose **Insert Row/Column** from the Edit Menu and then select **row** to insert a row.

   b. Choose **Delete Row/Column** from the Edit Menu and then select **column** to delete a column.

9. To insert or delete multiple rows or columns, you must first select the rows or columns with the **F8** key *before* you go to the Edit Menu. (Example: Using the **F8** key, select columns A and B and then complete the "insert" column commands).
10. Since this was for demonstration only, close the spreadsheet without saving it.

SECTION 2

Skills to be learned in this section

- Formatting cells
- Changing cell alignment
- Changing column width
- Copying cell contents
- Moving cell contents
- Using functions
- Using a relative reference
- Using an absolute reference

FORMATTING CELLS

You can change the appearance of numeric values by changing the cell's format. There are seven numeric formats:

General	7654.32
Dollar (2 dec.)	$7,654.32
Fixed (3 dec.)	7654.320
Comma (4 dec.)	7,654.3200
Percent (0 dec.)	765432%
Exponential (2 dec.)	7.65E+03
Logical	True/False

Do this:

1. Open a new spreadsheet and type **76.239** in cell Al and press **Enter.**

2. With the cursor still in cell A1, press **Alt** then type **t**.

3. In the Format Menu choose **Currency** then **2** decimal places (the number in cell A1 should now be $76.24).

4. Keep the spreadsheet open for the next drill.

CHANGING CELL ALIGNMENT

The contents can be aligned in the left, center, or right portion of the cell. Text is automatically left-aligned and numbers right-aligned when first entered.

Do this:

1. In a blank cell of the spreadsheet type **TITLE** and press **Enter**.
2. With the cursor still in that cell, press **Alt** then type **t**.
3. In the Format Menu choose **Style**.
4. Under alignment, select **center** and the word TITLE is centered in the cell.

CHANGING COLUMN WIDTH

The width of a column can be changed from 0 to 79 characters. The default width is 10 characters. To set it, use the Column Width command from the Format Menu.

Do this:

1. Type the number **12345** in a blank cell and press **Enter**.
2. With the cursor still in that column, press **Alt** then type **t**.
3. In the Format Menu choose **Column Width**.
4. Type **3** and press **Enter**. The column closes to 3 characters wide and the asterisks indicate the column is not wide enough to hold the size of the cell contents.
5. Repeat steps 2 and 3.
6. Type **15** and press **Enter**. The column quickly expands to accommodate 15 characters.
7. Close the spreadsheet file without saving it [**Alt-F-C**].

COPYING CELL CONTENTS

The Edit Menu gives you four commands for copying: Fill Right, Fill Down, Copy, and Copy Special. You use each command in different situations.

The copy command copies the selected cells' contents and format into other spreadsheet cells or other WORKS files. This makes it possible to type a formula once and copy it into several cells, making it faster to create a spreadsheet and reducing the chance for error.

The selected cells' contents and format replace the contents and format of the spreadsheet cells you are copying into. Copied relative references adjust for their new location.

Fill Right copies the first column of selected cells into the selected cells to the right.

Fill Down copies the first row of selected cells into the selected cells below.

Copy makes one copy of the selected cells on another part of the spreadsheet.

Copy Special adds or subtracts the selected cells to cells in another part of the spreadsheet, or copies just the values of the selected cells to another part of the spreadsheet, or converts a formula to its value.

Do this:

1. In a blank spreadsheet type **COPY THIS** into cell A1 and press **Enter.**
2. With the cursor still in A1 press **F8**, then press the **Right Arrow** to move the cursor to cell C1.
3. Press **Alt**, type **E**, then **R** to activate the "Fill Right" procedure.
4. The text in cell A1 has been copied to cells B1 and C1.
5. Close the spreadsheet file without saving it.

MOVING CELL CONTENTS

The Move command is like the Copy command except the content moved no longer remains where it originally was. Cell contents cannot be *moved* between files, only copied.

Do this:

1. Open a new spreadsheet and type **MOVE THIS** in cell A1.
2. With the cursor still in A1 press **F8**.

3. Press **Alt**, type **E**, then type **M** to activate the move procedure.

4. Move the cursor to cell A5 and press **Enter** (the text in A1 should move to A5 and cell A1 is empty).

5. Close the spreadsheet file without saving it.

USING FUNCTIONS

A function is a built-in calculation that is similar to an arithmetic operator, such as + or −, in that it produces a new value from other values.

Most functions consist of the function name, a set of parentheses, and arguments (the values the function uses to produce a new value) separated by commas. An argument must be a number or an expression that results in a number. This means that an argument can be a number, a cell or range reference, another function, or any combination.

> Example: SUM gives the total of all values in the references that may be numbers, cell references, range references, or formulas. In range references, blank cells are ignored. In cell references, blank cells are treated as zero. =SUM(B2:B6)

USING A RELATIVE REFERENCE

A formula refers to locations in the spreadsheet by cell references. If it is a relative reference, it is in relation to where the cell is located in the spreadsheet relative to where the formula is located. When the formula is copied or moved to another location, the cell reference adjusts automatically to the new location.

USING AN ABSOLUTE REFERENCE

To prevent a cell reference in a formula from automatically adjusting relative to new locations, make it an absolute reference. An absolute reference always refers to the same cell location in the spreadsheet even if the formula is copied or moved. To make it an absolute reference include a dollar sign in front of the column letter and in front of the row number. (Example: To make cell C6 absolute, type it as C6.)

41

DRILL-4

Tasks   This drill lets you practice the following:

- Formatting cells
- Entering formulas and functions
- Naming and saving a spreadsheet
- Printing a spreadsheet

Procedure   From the following information, complete the steps for DRILL-4.

If you have any problems, review the material in Chapter 3, Sections 1 and 2.

1. Open a new spreadsheet and enter the information below into the spreadsheet. Be sure the text and numbers are in the same cells as in the example.

	A	B	C	D
1		Month 1	Month 2	Month 3
2	Sales	30000	26000	34000
3	Profits	8000	6000	9500

2. Press **F8** to select the headings in cells B1, C1, and D1. Then use the **Format/Style** command and, in the "Alignment" box, change the alignment for the months to *center* and press **Enter**.

3. In cell E1, type **Totals**. Center it like the months were centered.

4. In cell E2, enter a *formula* that will cause cells B2, C2, and D2 to be added to give their sum. **=B2+C2+D2**

5. In cell E3, enter a *function* that will cause cells B3, C3, and D3 to be added to give their sum. **=SUM(B3:D3)**

6. Press **F8** to select cells E2 and E3. Use **Format/Style** to format the contents of those cells as "bold."

7. Using the **File/Save As** command, save the spreadsheet as PROFITS.WKS.

8. Use the **Print/Print** command and print out your spreadsheet.

9. Compare your printout to the key on the following page.

10. Close the spreadsheet.

KEY: DRILL-4
Chapter 3 - Section 2

	Month 1	Month 2	Month 3	Totals
Sales	30000	26000	34000	90000
Profits	8000	6000	9500	23500

DRILL-5

Tasks This drill lets you practice the following:

- Selecting a range
- Editing and formatting cells
- Copying and moving cells
- Saving and printing a spreadsheet

Procedure From the information below, complete the steps for DRILL-5.

If you have any problems, review the material in Chapter 3, Sections 1 and 2.

1. Open a new spreadsheet. Move the cursor to cell B1 and use the **Format/Column Width** command to widen that column from 10 to 20.

   a. *Formatting* The column headings of "Price" and "Extension" are to be aligned to the right and the amounts under "Quantity" are centered. Cells C4, D4, D9, and D12 should be formatted for "Currency." The range C5:D7 and cell D10 should be formatted "fixed" with two decimal places. You can set the format in cell C5, then select cells C5 through C7 and use the **Fill Down** command from the Edit Menu. You can repeat that procedure for the cells in column "D."

   b. *Entering* Enter the data as provided below. Be careful to enter it in the cells as shown. In cells A1, A3, and A8, type enough dashes to extend through column D. Include a quote at the beginning of the entry to signify text.

	A	B	C	D
1	--			
2	Quantity	Description	Price	Extension
3	--			
4	2	Boxes--file folders	$3.45	
5	4	Dozen--#2 pencils	0.98	
6	12	Legal pads	1.15	
7	3	Pencil sharpeners	9.95	
8	--			
9			Sub Total	
10			Tax (6%)	
11				----------
12			Total	

2. Now move to cell D2 and use the **Edit/Clear** commands to clear "Extension." Now type **Amount** in cell D2 and press **Enter**.

3. To arrive at the Amount for each column, enter a formula to multiply "Quantity" times "Price." Do that for cells D4 through D7.

   a. In cell D4, type in =A4*C4.

   b. With the cursor in cell D4, press **F8**.

   c. Using the **Down Arrow** move to cell D7.

   d. Press **Alt-E-F** to have the formula in cell D4 copied to the cells below.

4. Enter the formula **=SUM(D4:D7)** in cell D9 to add the amounts in column D.

5. Enter the formula **=D9*6%** in cell D10 to multiply the "Sub Total" by the tax rate.

6. Enter the formula **=D9+D10** in cell D12 to add the "Sub Total" and the "Tax."

7. Save it as INVOICE.WKS and get a printout.

8. Compare your printout to the key on the following page.

9. Close the spreadsheet file.

KEY: DRILL-5
Chapter 3 - Section 2

Quantity	Description	Price	Amount
2	Boxes--file folders	$3.45	$6.90
4	Dozen--#2 pencils	0.98	3.92
12	Legal pads	1.15	13.80
3	Pencil sharpeners	9.95	29.85
		Sub Total	$54.47
		Tax (6%)	3.27
		Total	$57.74

DRILL-6

Tasks This drill lets you practice the following:

- Recalling a spreadsheet
- Changing cell width and alignment
- Deleting and inserting
- Copying and clearing cell contents

Procedure From the information below, complete the steps for DRILL-6.

If you have any problems, review the material in Chapter 3, Sections 1 and 2.

1. Recall from your disk the spreadsheet called PROFITS.WKS that you saved from Drill-4.

2. In column A change the width to 14 and then in cell A4 type **Rate of Return.**

3. Type a formula for the "rate of return" (profits divided by sales would be =A3/A2) in cell B4 and then format it for percent (one decimal place). Now select range B4:E4 and use the **Fill Right** command from the Edit Menu to copy the formula to the other cells.

4. Select range A1:E4 and copy it to range A10:E13.

5. Select range B10:E13, then choose **Edit/Clear** to clear the contents of that range (this should remove the data but maintain the formatting).

6. Type the following:

cell B10:	**Month 1**
cell C10:	**Month 2**
cell D10:	**Month 3**
cell E10:	**Totals**

7. In cell A11 insert a row. Do the same for cell A2.

8. In cell A2 type in enough dashes to extend through column E (be careful to enter them as *text*). Now copy that line to cell A12.

9. Enter the following amounts for that quarter:

	Month 1	Month 2	Month 3
Sales	41000	38000	59000
Profits	11000	9800	16700

10. Move to cell E13 and use the **F8** key to select the range E13:E14. Now, while in E13, type this function, **=SUM(B13:D13)**, and press **Ctrl + Enter**. This will simultaneously enter the same function, adjusted for relative references, into all of the cells you selected.

11. Move to cell B15 and use the **F8** key to select the range B15:E15. Now, while in B15, type the formula needed **(=B14/B13)** and press **Ctrl + Enter**. This will simultaneously enter the same formula, adjusted for relative references, into all of the cells you selected.

12. Use the **Save** command to save it, then print it.

13. Compare your printout to the key on the following page.

14. Close the spreadsheet file.

KEY: DRILL-6
Chapter 3 - Section 2

	Month 1	Month 2	Month 3	Totals
Sales	30000	26000	34000	**90000**
Profits	8000	6000	9500	**23500**
Rate of Return	26.7%	23.1%	27.9%	26.1%

	Month 1	Month 2	Month 3	Totals
Sales	41000	38000	59000	**138000**
Profits	11000	9800	16700	**37500**
Rate of Return	26.8%	25.8%	28.3%	27.2%

SECTION 3 (Charts)

Skills to be learned in this section

- Components of charts
- Creating "speed" charts
- Formatting and customizing charts
- Viewing and naming charts
- Saving and printing charts

COMPONENTS OF CHARTS

A chart is generated from spreadsheet data. Charting turns spreadsheet information into a picture which makes it easier to understand and remember. Each spreadsheet can have up to eight separate charts attached to it. Each time the data in the spreadsheet is changed, the charts automatically change too. WORKS also allows eight different *types* of charts to be created. The line, bar, and pie chart types are the most frequently used.

Except for pie charts, the other types all have a Y-axis and an X-axis. Pie charts are circles that have "slices" instead of a Y-axis and an X-axis. The Y-axis is a vertical line where the *values* of the spreadsheet are displayed. The X-axis is a horizontal line where the values are *named* (labeled).

Chart Component	Menu & Option Needed
Chart Title	Data/Titles
Subtitle	Data/Titles
X-Axis Title	Data/Titles
Y-Axis Title	Data/Titles
Legends	Data/Legends
Gridlines	Options/X-Axis
Gridlines	Options/Y-Axis
Border	Options/Show Border
Title Font	Format/Title Font

When you access the View Menu you can select a specific chart to view, create a new chart, or go to the "Charts" dialog box. When you create a new chart, WORKS assigns it a name. (Example: Chart1, Chart2, etc.)

After viewing a chart, you are automatically returned to the *Chart* screen. If in doubt whether you are viewing the chart screen or the spreadsheet screen, just look on the next-to-last line and it will say "CHART" if you are in the chart screen. You can return to the spreadsheet screen by using the Spreadsheet command in the View Menu or by using the F10 shortcut keystroke.

When you select Charts from the View Menu, you will be in a Charts dialog box where you can Rename, Delete or Copy a previous chart (see below).

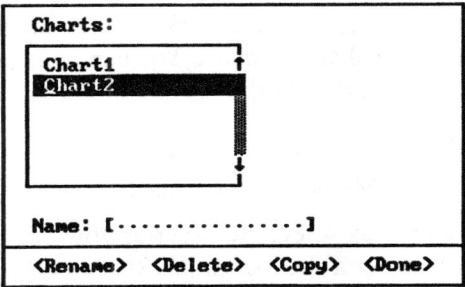

CREATING "SPEED" CHARTS

When the ranges to be charted are adjacent to each other, you can let WORKS create a "speed" chart for you. The Y-series that is used is based on the shape of the range you select in the spreadsheet. WORKS automatically creates a bar chart if you do not select a specific type.

Do this:

1. In a blank spreadsheet type the following:

	A	B	C	D
1		**Larry**	**Moe**	**Curley**
2		**$15,000**	**$6,000**	**$9,000**
3				

2. Using the **F8** key, select range A1:D2.

3. From the View Menu choose **New Chart**. The chart is displayed on the screen.

4. Press **Esc** to leave the view screen mode. The shortcut key to view the chart is Shift + F10.

FORMATTING AND CUSTOMIZING CHARTS

One Y-series is created for each value selected. Each Y-series will appear in a chart as a separate line, bar, marker, or pie slice. (**Note:** You can delete a Y-series by using the Series list box in the Data Menu. Select the Y-series you want to delete and select the Delete option.)

WORKS uses colors, patterns, and markers to create a special format for each line, bar, or pie slice in a chart. You can include titles, legends, borders, and gridlines in the chart.

To Format a Y-series

1. From the Format Menu, choose Data Format.

2. In the Series list box select the Y-series you want to format. (If it is a pie chart, select a slice from the Slices box.)

3. Select the options you want from the Colors, Patterns, or Markers boxes. (**Note:** The options you have depends on the type of chart you have selected. Also, if you want WORKS to choose an option for you, select "Auto" in any list box.)

4. Choose Format to apply the selected options. (If you choose Format All, WORKS applies the selected options to all Y-series or pie slices.)

CREATING BORDERS

To have a border drawn around a chart, go to the Options Menu and select the Show Border command. You can select or deselect the same way.

SHOWING GRIDLINES

Gridlines run parallel to the X-axis and Y-axis and make the charted spreadsheet values easier to read. When you create a chart, the gridlines are initially turned off.

1. From the Options Menu, choose X-Axis or Y-Axis.
2. To show the gridlines, turn on the Grid Lines check box and press Enter. Turning this box off hides them.

VIEWING A CHART

To view a chart on the screen before saving it or printing it, select the View Menu and then the chart number (the shortcut key to view is Shift + F10). You can view a chart from either the spreadsheet screen or from the chart screen. Pressing any key allows you to leave the view screen mode.

NAMING A CHART

WORKS automatically assigns a name when a new chart is created. You can rename it either from the Chart Menu or the spreadsheet menu.

1. From the View Menu, choose Charts.
2. In the list box, select the chart you want to name.
3. In the "Name" text box, type in the new chart name.
4. Press the Rename button.

SAVING A CHART

You save a chart by saving the spreadsheet it is attached to. It is best to rename the chart in the chart screen before you save the spreadsheet. You save a spreadsheet the same way as a word processor file. Choose the File Menu and the Save or Save As command. You can do this from the chart screen or from the spreadsheet screen.

PRINTING A CHART

You can only print a chart from the chart screen. The normal Print/Print commands are used. Before you print, check the View Menu to see which chart is the active chart. The active chart will have a *bullet* in front of its name in the View Menu box. If the chart you want to print is not the active chart, view it and when you press Esc, it will now be the active chart.

DRILL-7

Tasks   This drill lets you practice the following:

- "Speed" charting
- Changing chart types
- Exploding a pie slice
- Renaming a chart
- Deleting a chart
- Printing a chart
- Saving a spreadsheet with a chart attached

Procedure   From the information below, complete the steps for DRILL-7.

If you have any problems, review the material in Chapter 3, Section 3.

1. Open the spreadsheet PROFITS.WKS.
2. If you have a line in row 2, *delete* that row. Use **Edit/Delete** a *row*, and then select the range A1:D3.
3. Choose **View/New Chart**. Then press **Esc** to go back to the chart screen.
4. Choose **View/Charts**.

5. Tab to the Name box and type **Sales & Profits** and press **Enter.** Then press **Alt-D** to record the new name.

6. From the chart screen use the Print Menu to get a printout.

7. Select range A3:D3.

8. Choose **View/New Chart** then press **Esc** to go back to the chart screen.

9. Choose **View/2.** Press **Esc** to return to the chart screen.

10. Choose **View/Charts.** Position the selection bar over Chart 1. Tab to the Delete brackets and press **Enter.** Then answer "OK" to delete Chart 1. Press **Esc** to return to the chart screen.

11. Choose **Format/Pie** to change the chart type.

12. Choose **View/1** to view the "pie" chart, then press **Esc** to return to the chart screen.

13. Choose **Format/Data Format** and press **Alt-E** to turn on the "exploded" feature. Press **Enter** to record it. Press **Alt-D** because you are "done" formatting the data.

14. Go view the chart again. Then press **Esc** and use the Print Menu in the chart screen to get a printout of the exploded pie chart.

15. Save and close the spreadsheet.

16. Compare your printouts to the keys on the following pages.

KEY #1: DRILL 7

KEY #2: DRILL 7

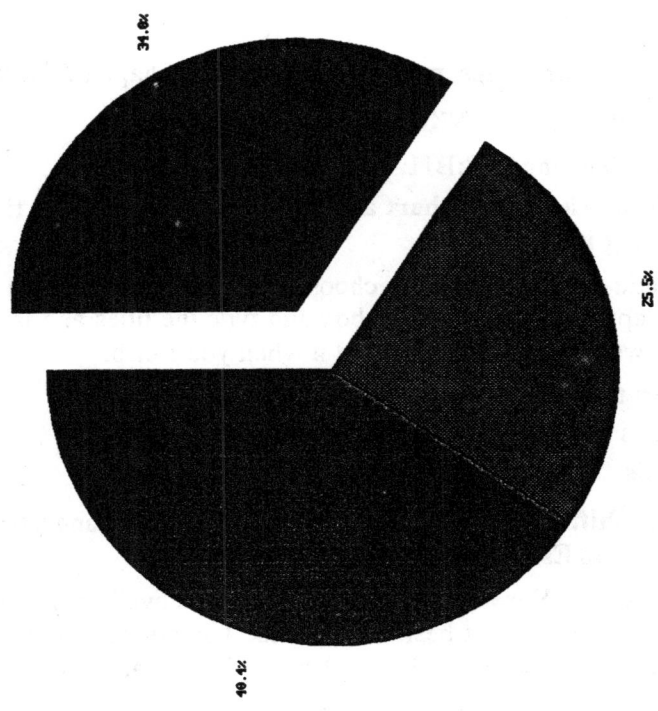

DRILL-8

Tasks   This drill lets you practice the following:

- Adding a title
- Naming a chart
- Copying a chart

Procedure   From the information below, complete the steps for DRILL-8.

If you have any problems, review the material in Chapter 3, Section 3.

1. Open the STOCK.WKS spreadsheet.
2. Select the range A8:B11.
3. Choose **View/New Chart** and press **Esc** when you are finished viewing it.
4. To add titles and legends choose **Data/Titles**. When the Titles box appears, move to each box and type the titles and labels as follows. Press **Enter** to record it when you finish.

Chart title	**Portfolio of Stocks**
X-axis	**Stocks Held**
Y-axis	**Dollars**

5. Press **Shift + F10** to see how it looks with the titles and labels and then press **Esc** when you have seen it.
6. Choose the **View** Menu and notice the "active" chart you just viewed has a bullet beside it. Choose **Charts**, tab to the Name box, type **Portfolio**, and press **Enter**. That renames the chart.
7. Tab to the Copy brackets and press **Enter** to make a *duplicate* of the active chart. Notice the name of the new chart and then press **Esc.**
8. Choose the **View** Menu and notice that the new chart you just made from the other chart now has the bullet by it, indicating it is now the active chart. Using this View Menu, alternate making these last two charts the active one and go view each to see that they are in fact duplicates.
9. Be sure the Portfolio chart is active, print it, and save the spreadsheet.
10. Compare your printout to the key on the following page.

KEY: DRILL 8

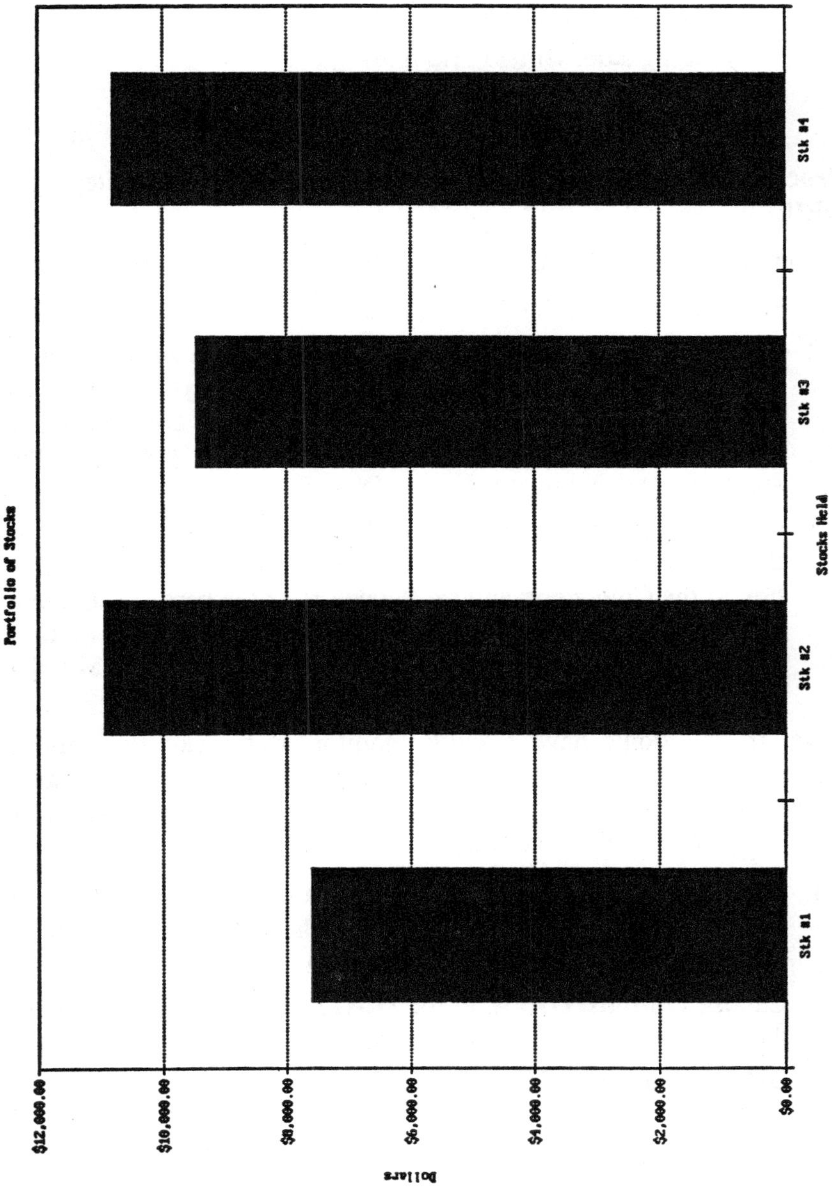

Portfolio of Stocks

Stk #4

Stk #3

Stocks Held

Stk #2

Stk #1

$12,000.00

$10,000.00

$8,000.00

$6,000.00

$4,000.00

$2,000.00

$0.00

Dollars

DRILL-9

Tasks   This drill lets you practice the following:

- Recalling a chart
- Changing colors and patterns
- Adding a border and grid lines
- Changing the orientation of a chart
- Changing the size of a chart

Procedure   From the information below, complete the steps for DRILL-9.

If you have any problems, review the material in Chapter 3, Section 3.

1. Open the STOCK.WKS spreadsheet.

2. Choose **View/Portfolio** to view it and make it the active chart. It should be the same chart that was active when you saved it as "Portfolio" in Drill-8. This illustrates how charts are attached to the spreadsheets they were built from when you save the spreadsheet they are attached to. Press **Esc**.

3. Choose **Format/Data Format** and set the colors and patterns for the bars for the chart named Portfolio. You move from the Series box to the Colors box and set the color for the bars. Then move to the Patterns box and set the pattern for the bars. Press **Alt-A <Format All>** to record it, then **Alt-D <Done>** to leave the dialog box.

Note: If you don't have a color monitor, just make the pattern different. Experiment with the patterns available and go view the new bar patterns each time. When you have finished experimenting, select the "==" pattern as the final one.

4. Choose **Options/Show Border** to put a border on the chart. To visually see what was done, go view the chart after each step. Then press **Esc** to perform the next step.

5. Choose **Options/Y-Axis**. Press **Alt-G** and then **Enter** to turn on the Grid Lines box and leave the menu.

6. Get a printout of the chart.

7. Choose **Print/Page Setup and Margins** and change the chart orientation from *Landscape* to *Portrait*. Although it will not show on your screen, this will cause the chart to be printed vertically instead of the normal horizontal way. Still in the Page Setup and Margins dialog box, change the "Chart height" from 9 inches to 5 inches and change the "Chart width" from 6 inches to 7 inches. Press **Enter** to record the changes.

8. Print the chart and save the spreadsheet.

9. Compare your printouts to the keys on the following pages.

10. Close the spreadsheet file.

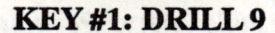

KEY #1: DRILL 9

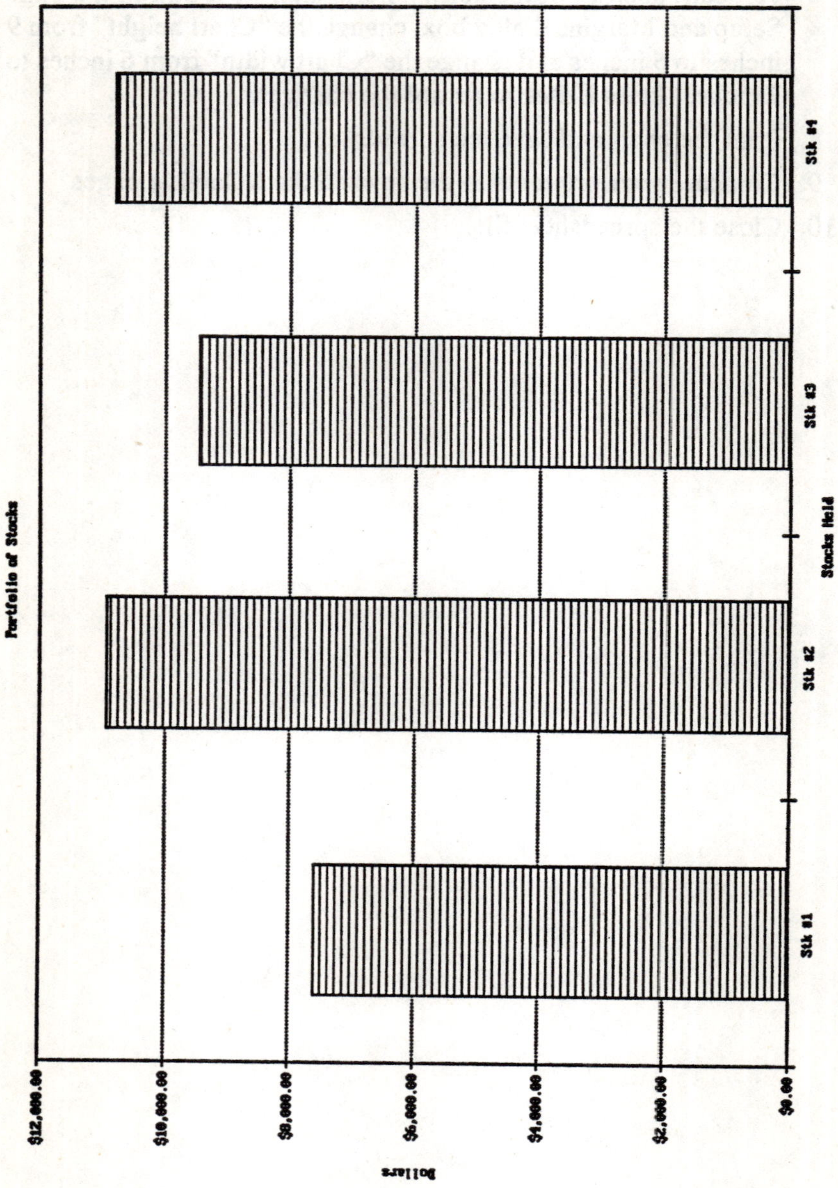

Portfolio of Stocks

(chart)

KEY #2: DRILL 9

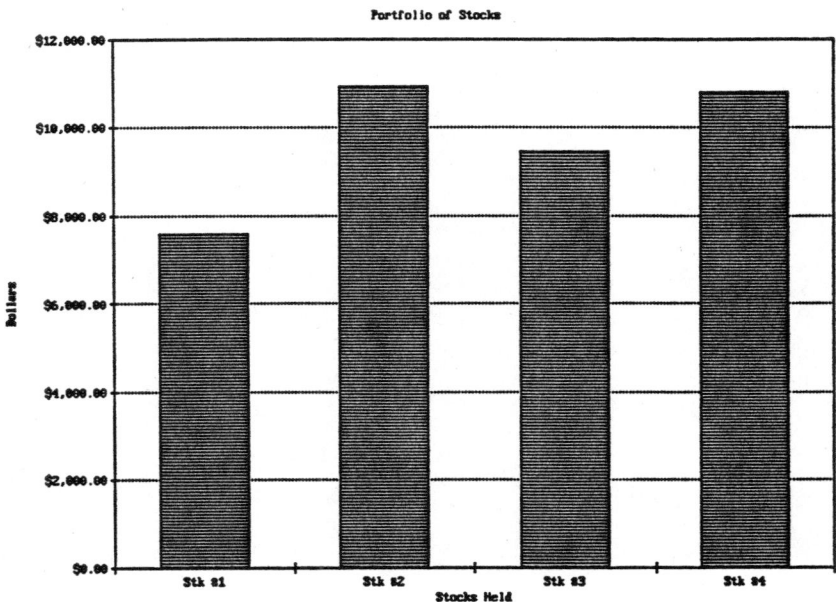

Chapter 4

DATABASE

The database serves as a computerized filing system. It can sort entries, copy, move, change, find and organize the data alphabetically or numerically.

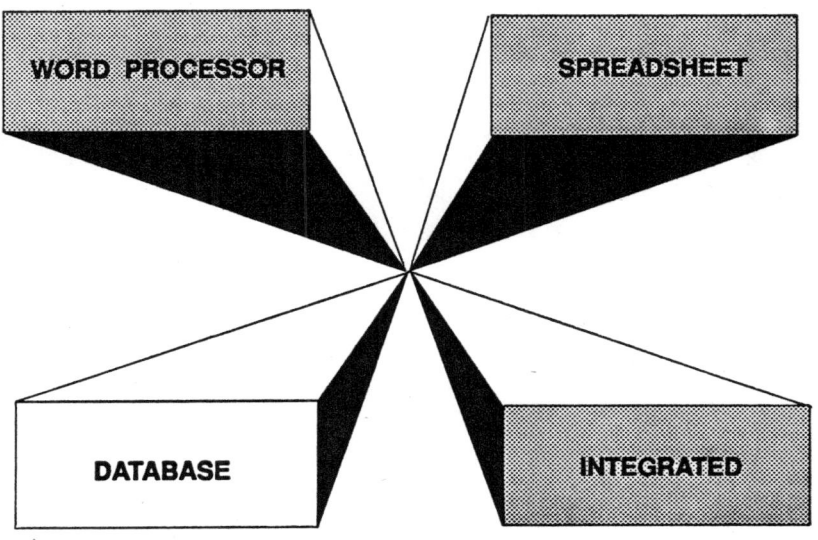

SECTION 1

Skills to be learned in this section

- Introducing a database
- Designing and creating a database
- Creating fields and labels
- Setting the field size
- Formatting numbers in a field
- Editing a database
- Moving in the database

INTRODUCING THE DATABASE

A database is a computerized record-keeping system that organizes and structures the data so it can be easily manipulated and retrieved. It is an electronic file cabinet—a place to store, scan, search, sort, and select information. It lets you arrange and rearrange information at will, scan records selected, and merge information with just a few keystrokes.

The WORKS database structures data in the form of a table that is similar to the spreadsheet. Within that structure, you should plan in advance

- what fields it should contain
- the order of the fields
- the name of each field
- the width of each field

This careful preplanning will enable you to enter the information into the database more easily. The structure can be changed later, however, if needed.

Database Definitions

Character   A letter, symbol, number, or blank space. [Joe Jones] = 9 characters and [A-123] = 5 characters.

Entry (Cell)   An individual piece of information, such as the last name "Smith" or a product description "Green Widgets."

Field Contents   One type of information, such as all the last names in a database. Each *column* in WORKS represents a field.

Field Formula   A formula entered in a field instead of a value or a label. The calculation is based on data entered in other fields of the same record.

Field Name   The name for the type of data to be entered. Each *column* in the file has a field name.

File   A collection of all records, the database itself.

Label   Descriptions, instructions, and any text that helps to clarify the form but doesn't allow data entry.

Record   All information about a particular subject, such as the last name, first name, address, and phone number of a particular person. Each row in WORKS represents a record.

Query   An instruction or set of instructions entered into a field or several fields that causes WORKS to search the entire database (including hidden records) in an attempt to match the criterion you have entered.

DESIGNING AND CREATING A DATABASE

Creating a database involves the three major activities of design, input, and output.

Design   It is important to plan in advance. Get your objectives clearly in mind before you start. Think about the kind and quantity of information you want to store and the types of reports you want to generate. Then use the Form screen to create the design and to name and position the fields and labels that make up your form. A form can be up to eight screens long. Once the form is created, it is used to enter the information into your database.

Input   This involves entering the data in the fields you create and adding, updating, and deleting the data as needed.

Output   The output is the screen and the printed reports. You can vary the content and appearance by arranging the records in alphabetical, numerical, or chronological order.

The Basic Steps in Database Creation and Use

1. Type the data into the database using the Form view.
2. Use Format/Style to add emphasis to words or change the alignment.
3. Use Format/Field Width to change the width of a field.
4. See several records at one time by going to the List view screen (press F9).
5. Sort the records in a different order by using the Select/Sort Records command.
6. Find specific records by using the View/Query command.
7. Save a database by using the File/Save As command.
8. Print a database by using the Print/Print command.

Once the form has been created, you can change the size and formatting of fields and enter and edit field names, field contents, and labels. You can move or copy fields, field contents, or a label and insert or delete a field or a label.

WORKS lets you look at the records and fields in two ways: on the *Form* screen or on the *List* screen. The Form screen shows one record at a time. The List screen shows many records at one time.

You can organize forms so they look like printed documents by using the Form screen. You position text anywhere you want on the screen to create the form into which you can enter data. On this screen you can also include explanatory text called labels. You do not have to enter something in every field. There can be a partial record in a database and the empty fields can be filled in later. Each field must have a unique name so data in different fields can be distinguished from each other.

To move from field contents to field contents in the Form screen, press the Tab key. When you press Tab in the *last* field of a record, the *first* field of the next record appears.

CREATING FIELDS

The Form screen is used to lay out the names and labels that make up the database form. A field on the Form screen contains two parts: the *field name* and the *field contents*. The field name describes the data in the field. A field name can be up to 15 characters long and must be followed by a colon (:). SINGLE QUOTATION MARKS ARE NOT ALLOWED IN A FIELD NAME. The field names you create on the Form screen appear across the top of the List screen. When you enter a field name and then the colon, WORKS then asks you what width you want for the field. **CAUTION:** Do *not* try to make your own lines after the colon in the field name. It will be interpreted as a "label" and you won't be able to make entries in it.

Note: You can also create a new field in the List view by moving the cursor into an unnamed column and typing an entry. WORKS gives these field names, Field1, Field2, etc.. You can then use Edit/Field Name to change the name.

SETTING THE FIELD SIZE

A field can be 25 characters wide and 2 lines high in Form view and 40 characters wide in List view. You set the field size separately for each view. Initially, every cell is 20 characters wide. You select the width when you design the field. It can be changed later if needed. The height of a cell is 1 line unless you want multiple-line fields.

CREATING LABELS

You can use labels for such things as titles or instructions. Labels do not hold data. A label can be any text as long as the last character is *not* a colon. YOU CANNOT ENTER OR EDIT LABELS IN LIST VIEW. Proper preplanning includes determining any *formulas* you want to use in the Form screen. These formulas make use of the field names you used when designing the screen. Any names in your formulas that are not *exactly* like your field names are not accepted when you enter the formula. If this happens, either change the formula to agree with the field names, or go back to the Form screen and make the field names the same as what you want to use in your formula.

CREATING FIELDS AND
LABELS IN THE FORM SCREEN

In the Form screen you have one record per form. You move the cursor to where you want the field or label and then type the field name or the label. When you press Enter for a field, you are prompted to set the width of that field.

Repeat this procedure for every label and field you want in your form. When you are finished designing the form, you can enter information into your database.

An example of a very basic database form is shown below. Look at it and then follow the steps below to learn how to construct it.

```
                    FORM DESIGN EXAMPLE

   Last Name:     _____

   First Name:     _____

   Sales:  _____   Sales Tax:  _____   Total:  _____
```

Do this:

1. From the File Menu, choose **Create New File.**

2. In the New dialog box, select **New Database.**

3. Using the arrow keys, move down 2 spaces and to the right 20 spaces and type **FORM DESIGN EXAMPLE** and press **Enter.**

4. Press **Home,** move down a few spaces, type **Last Name:** and press **Enter,** and then type **25** in the Width text bracket and press **Enter.**

5. Move down again and type **First Name:** and press **Enter,** and then press **Enter** again to accept the default width of 20.

6. Move down again and type **Sales:** and press **Enter,** and then type a width of **9** and press **Enter.**

7. Move to the *right* a few spaces and type **Sales Tax:** and press **Enter,** then type a width of **9** and press **Enter.**

8. Move to the *right* a few spaces and type **Total:** and press **Enter,** then type a width of **9** and press **Enter.**

9. Select **Save As** from the File Menu and save it as DATATEST.WDB.

Note: Leave this database file open for use in the following pages.

FORMATTING NUMBERS IN A FIELD

WORKS has several formats that can be applied to numbers in a database: general, fixed, currency, comma, percent, and others. You can type and format a number at the same time, or the format can be set after the number is typed by using the Format Menu.

Do this:

1. Using the database you just designed, DATATEST.WDB, move the cursor to the Last Name field and type **Newton**.

2. Press the **Tab** key to move to the First Name field and type **Robert.**

3. Tab to the next field and enter the sales amount of **395.45** and press **Enter.**

4. While still in the Sales field, choose **Format/Currency** (with **2** decimal places), and now each time an amount is entered into this field, it will be formatted as currency.

Note: You could have entered the sales amount as $395.45 and the database would *automatically* format the field as currency since that was how you entered it.

5. Choose **View/List** to display the database layout in the List view.

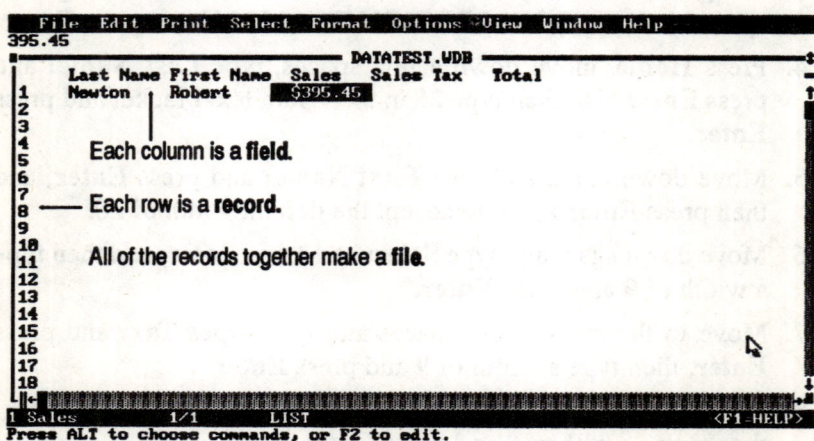

EDITING A DATABASE

Editing is necessary to correct errors and to update or replace the contents of a record with more current information. You can edit any field by selecting it and then pressing the F2 key.

MOVING IN THE DATABASE

The way you move around in the List view and Form view is about the same:

To move to the	In Form view press	In List view press
Leftmost field	Home	Home
Rightmost field	End	End
Next field	Tab	Tab
First record	Ctrl + Home	Ctrl + Home
Last record	Ctrl + End	Ctrl + End
Next record	Ctrl + PgDn	
Previous record	Ctrl + PgUp	

Moving Between the Form and List Screens

Pressing F9 will shuttle you between the Form and List screens.

SECTION 2

Skills to be learned in this section

- Entering text, numbers, and field formulas
- Printing the database
- Inserting blank lines or columns
- Moving a field
- Deleting records or fields

THE FORMULA BAR

Like the spreadsheet, you use the formula bar to enter text, numbers, and field formulas. What you type into the database is first displayed in the formula bar. Pressing Enter places the entry in the active cell.

ENTERING TEXT

Text can be any information that is not a number or formula. Numbers can be entered as text as long as you precede them with quotes ("). If you enter text that is longer than the width of a cell, WORKS displays as much of the text as possible. You could enter up to 256 characters.

A. **Making entries from the Forms screen**

1. Tab to the field you want to make an entry into.
2. In the formula bar, type the text and press Enter.

B. **Making entries from the List screen**

1. Move to the row for the record you want.
2. Tab to the field you want and make the entry.

Note: At the end of a record, press the Down Arrow and then the Home key to return to the first field of the next record.

ENTERING NUMBERS

Numbers are entered without a prefix. If you put quotation marks in front of a number, it will be interpreted as a label and cannot be manipulated by a formula.

Do this:

1. Using the DATATEST.WDB file again, make sure you are in the List screen.

2. Move to the "Last Name" field on row two and enter this information:

   Johnson   **John**   **55.80**

3. At the end of the row press **Down Arrow** and then **Home** to return to the first field of the next record.

4. Now for records #3 and #4 type the following:
   Burns   **Dorothy**   **126.50**
   McCrary   **Lloyd**   **9.99**

5. Press **F9** to switch back to the Form screen and you see *4/4* at the bottom of the screen, indicating you are now in form #4 of a total of 4 forms in the database.

ENTERING FIELD FORMULAS

A field formula is an equation that calculates a new value from existing fields. For example, the formula *=sales+tax* adds the values in the fields named "sales" and "tax." You can include in field formulas only field names from the *same* record. The formula can be entered into *any* record and the database will automatically update all of the other records in that field.

Do this:

1. Move to the "Sales Tax" field in any record in the Form screen of the DATATEST.WDB file and enter this formula: **=Sales * .06.**

2. Choose **Format/Currency**, with **2** decimal places, and notice the other records have the "Sales Tax" calculated too.

3. Now press **F9** to move to the List screen and Tab to the "Total" field.

4. Type in the formula, **=Sales + Sales Tax,** and press **Enter,** and you can see all of the records updated for that field at the same time.

5. While still in the "Total" field, choose **Format/Currency** with **2** decimal places and again you can see all records formatted at the same time.

PRINTING THE DATABASE

In Form view you can print just what is on the screen. If you move to a *blank form,* just the field names and labels will be printed. In List view you can print what appears on the screen, just the field contents, or you can print the field names and record numbers *with* the field contents.

Do this:

1. Make sure that the database file, DATATEST.WDB, is the current file and choose **Print/Print.**

2. From the Print dialog box you can select from the following options: more than one copy, print certain pages only, print to file, and print record and field labels. Type **2** in the "Number of copies:" brackets and press **Enter.** That should cause the database file to be printed twice.

INSERTING BLANK LINES OR COLUMNS

You can insert a blank line between fields in the Form screen or a blank column (or row) in the List screen.

A. **In the Form screen**

1. Move the cursor to where you want the new line inserted.

2. Go to the Edit Menu and choose the Insert Line command.

3. A blank line is inserted and all of the fields below the inserted line move down one line.

B. **In the List screen**

1. Move the cursor to the column where you want a new column (field) inserted.
2. Go to the Edit Menu and choose the Insert Record/Field option.
3. In the dialog box, select "field" and press Enter. The column the cursor is on is moved one column to the right and the new column appears.

MOVING A FIELD

You can move a field at any time. If you start a move, you can cancel it by pressing Esc.

A. **Move a Field in Form View**   In this view you can move a field or a label.

1. Move the cursor to the label or the field you want to move.
2. Press F3 (the shortcut "move" key).
3. Move to where you want the label or field located and press Enter.

B. **Move a Field in List View**   You can move a field only after it is selected. More than one field can be moved at one time in this view.

1. Move the cursor to the top of the field to be moved and choose Select/Field.
2. Press F3 (the shortcut "move" key).
3. Move the cursor to the top of the field that you want the move to be placed in front of (the field you moved is inserted to the *left* of the field in which the cursor was placed).
4. Press Enter.

Note: When you *move* a field in the Form view, it is *not* moved in the List view (and vice versa). Also, when you *add* a field name to the List view, the field is placed at the "bottom" in the Form view. A field *added* in the Form view will be placed at the "end" in the List view. If you want the order of both views to be identical, you must move the fields after they are added.

DELETING A RECORD

You can delete a record in either the Form screen or the List screen.

A. **In the Form screen**   Just use the Delete Record option in the Edit Menu and that record is deleted.

B. **In the List screen**
   1. Put your cursor in the record (row) you want deleted.
   2. Choose Delete Record/Field from the Edit Menu.
   3. In the dialog box select Record and press Enter.

DELETING A FIELD

Field deletions can take place in the Form screen or the List screen.

A. **In the Form screen**
   1. Place the cursor on the field name to be deleted.
   2. Choose Edit/Delete Field.
   3. WORKS then asks if it's OK to delete the data in the field.
   4. Pressing Enter deletes the field and its contents.

B. **In the List screen**
   1. Put the cursor in the field to delete.
   2. Choose Delete Record/Field from the Edit Menu, then in the dialog box select Field and press Enter.

   Note: You can use F8 to select several fields to delete at one time.

Do this:

1. Move to the List screen in the DATATEST.WDB file.

2. Press **Ctrl-Home** to be sure the cursor is in the top left cell and choose **Edit/Insert Record/Field,** and select the "field" option.

3. Place the cursor in row 1 of the First Name field, choose **Select/Field,** and the field to be moved is highlighted. Now press **F3** (the shortcut *move* key).

4. Move the cursor to the newly opened column and press **Enter,** and all of the records are moved to the first column.

5. Move back to the now empty column and delete it (**Edit/Delete Record/Field** and choose the "field" option).

DRILL-10

Tasks   This drill lets you practice the following:

- Designing a database
- Changing field width
- Entering data
- Saving a database
- Printing a database

Procedure   From the information below, complete the steps for DRILL-10.

If you have any problems, review the material in Chapter 4, Sections 1 and 2.

1. Create a new database and design it as follows. The Name field should have a *width* of 18; all others should have a width of 10 (leave height = 1 for all of the fields). Also, format the Pay Rate and Gross Pay fields as *currency*, with 2 decimal places.

   Move the cursor down 5 lines and to the right about 15 spaces to begin the form. Then duplicate the layout below (single spaced).

   Weekly Payroll

   ```
   -----------------------------------
   Name:   _____
   Reg Hours:  _____
   O/T Hours:  _____
   Pay Rate:   _____
   Gross Pay:  _____
   ```

2. When you finish the form design, get a printout of the blank form (from the Form screen, choose **Print/Print**).

3. Tab to the contents for the Gross Pay field and enter this *field formula*:

   =(Reg Hours * Pay Rate)+(O/T Hours * Pay Rate * 1.5)

4. Starting in the first field in record number one in the Form screen, enter these 3 records:

	Record 1	Record 2	Record 3
Name:	Joe Smith	Mary Johnson	Gayle McCrary
Reg Hours:	40	35	40
O/T Hours:	3.5	0	2
Pay Rate:	7.50	3.90	5.75

5. While still in the Form screen and on record number 3, get a printout of a completed form.

6. Press **F9** to move to the List screen. Move to the Name field and use **Format/Field Width** to widen that field to 18 in this screen too. Use **Print/Page Setup & Margins** to make *both* the left and right margins 1 inch. Now get a printout that shows field names and record numbers. Use **Print/Print record and field labels**.

7. Save it as PAYROLL.WDB.

8. Compare the printouts to the key on the following page.

```
╔═══════════════════════════════════════════════════╗
║  ┌─────────────────────────────────────────────┐  ║
║  │            KEY: DRILL-10                      │  ║
║  │          Chapter 4 - Section 2                │  ║
║  └─────────────────────────────────────────────┘  ║
```

1ST PRINTOUT

```
                      Weekly Payroll
          ---------------------------
          Name:
          Reg Hours:
          O/T Hours:
          Pay Rate:
          Gross Pay:
```

2ND PRINTOUT

```
                      Weekly Payroll
          ---------------------------
          Name: Gayle McCrary
          Reg Hours:            40
          O/T Hours:             2
          Pay Rate:        $5.75
          Gross Pay:     $247.25
```

3RD PRINTOUT

	Name	Reg Hours	O/T Hours	Pay Rate	Gross Pay
1	Joe Smith	40	3.5	$7.50	$339.38
2	Mary Johnson	35	0	$3.90	$136.50
3	Gayle McCrary	40	2	$5.75	$247.25

SECTION 3

Skills to be learned in this section

- Using the "Go To" command
- Using the "Search" command
- Locking and unlocking protected fields
- Proposing a field's contents with a formula
- Sorting records
- Hiding and showing records and fields
- Inserting page breaks in Form view and List view

USING THE GO TO COMMAND

This command allows you to go immediately to a field name or record number.

1. From the Select Menu choose Go To.

2. The dialog box lists all of the database field names.

3. Type the record number or field name, and the cursor zips to that record.

USING THE SEARCH COMMAND

This command allows you to find data that is entered in the records as "text."

1. From the Select Menu choose Search.

2. Type into the "Search for" dialog box all or part of something that you know is in the record you want.

3. WORKS then searches *below* where the cursor is positioned in the database until it finds the first entry matching the search information.

4. Each time you press F7 it continues the search.

Note: It will "loop" the database and continue the search as long as you continue to press F7.

LOCKING AND UNLOCKING PROTECTED FIELDS

To keep from accidentally erasing or changing the contents of a field, WORKS allows you to lock out changes by turning on the protect option. All fields are initially locked, but *not* protected until you turn the protection feature on. This causes all locked fields to be protected, but all unlocked fields are still unprotected.

Use **Options/Protect Form** to protect the design of the form. This denies changes to the *design* of the form, but allows changes to the *contents* of the fields.

Use **Options/Protect Data** to protect the field contents. This denies access to the *content* in fields that are locked.

The **Protect** command turns protection on and off. Since all fields are initially locked, you should unlock all fields whose contents you want to edit when the protection is turned on. Protecting fields is a two-step process.

A. **To Unlock Fields**
1. Using the F8 key, select the field(s) you want to unlock (these will be the fields you *can* change while protection is on).
2. Choose Format/Style and remove the "X" in the Locked check box and press Enter.

B. **To Protect Fields**
From the Options Menu choose Protect Form or Protect Data. A dot beside the command means it is turned on. When it is turned on, you can Tab only to the unlocked fields. It skips over all locked fields.

PROPOSING A FIELD'S CONTENTS WITH A FORMULA

If you have a field where the content will be the same from record to record, you can cause WORKS to automatically enter the content for you. To do this, type the text with a formula, then in succeeding records that field will automatically be the same. If you then want something else, just type it in as usual.

Example: If you want the "State" field to be *Texas*, type ="Texas" in the first record and it will be in the "state" field for all succeeding records.

SORTING RECORDS

Sorts can be alphabetically, numerically, and chronologically. The fields you want to sort are called *key fields*. In the dialog box for the Sort command, there is a place for the names of three key fields and the order of each field: ascending (A to Z, 1 to 9, or earliest date to the latest) or descending (Z to A, 9 to 1, or latest date to the earliest).

1. Choose Select/Sort Records.

2. In the 1st Field text box, type the name of the first field you want to sort.

3. Select either Ascend or Descend.

4. Repeat steps 2 and 3 for the second and third fields to be sorted (if wanted) and press Enter.

Sort Examples

Descending Sort (DOWN)

Numbers	Dates	Letters
26	1990	Z
25	1989	Y
24	1988	X
.	.	.
.	.	.
3	1975	C
2	1974	B
1	1973	A

Ascending Sort (UP)

HIDING RECORDS

Hidden records are not displayed in the List view and they cannot be printed or included in a report. The Status line shows how many records are showing of the total number of records available. (Example: If 5 records out of 25 are hidden, the Status line shows 20/25.)

1. Select the record you want to hide (you can select more than one record at a time in the List screen).
2. Choose Select/Hide Record.

Note: You can interchange the "hidden" and "showing" records by choosing Select/Switch Hidden Records.

HIDING FIELDS

Data in a field can be hidden in the List view. This allows more fields to be displayed.

1. Move the cursor to the field you want to hide.
2. Choose Format/Field Width and type zero (0).
3. Press Enter.

DISPLAYING A HIDDEN FIELD

You can redisplay a field that was previously hidden.

1. Choose Select/Go To.
2. In the Go To box, type the name of the field you want to display and press Enter.
3. Choose Format/Field Width.
4. Type a value greater than zero (0) and press Enter.

INSERTING PAGE BREAKS

When you have more information in your database than can be printed on one page, you can set your own page breaks. Like in the word processor, a page break mark (>>) appears. You can set separate page break marks in Form view than you set in List view and they will not affect each other.

A. Page Break in Form View

1. Put the cursor in the cell where you want the page break to begin.
2. Choose Print/Insert Page Break, and the page break marks ">>" appear to the left of that line.

B. Page Break in List View

1. Put the cursor in the row or field where you want the page break to begin.
2. Choose Print/Insert Page Break.
3. Select Row for a horizontal page break or Field for a vertical page break.
4. Choose OK and press Enter. The page break mark ">>" appears next to the *row* or *on top* of the field.

Note: To *delete* a page break, move the cursor to the cell, row, or field containing the page break marker and choose Print/Delete Page Break.

DRILL-11

Tasks   This drill lets you practice the following:

- Changing the field "height"
- Moving fields
- Adding labels, fields, and records
- Proposing a field's contents with a formula

Procedure   From the information below, complete the steps for DRILL-11.

If you have any problems, review the material in Chapter 4, Sections 2 and 3.

1. Open the file, PAYROLL.WDB, that you saved in DRILL-10.

2. In the List screen, move the cursor to the first record in the Reg Hours field. Press **F8** and extend the selection one column to the right. Now choose **Edit/Insert Record/Field.** Then select **Field** and press **Enter.** This should have inserted two empty columns between the Name field and the Reg Hours field to make room for the new field names to be added.

3. Put the cursor in the first empty column (field) you just created and choose **Edit/Field Name.** In the Name box type **Emp.No.,** and press **Enter.**

4. Move to the next empty column and do the same thing by naming that field **Dept.**

5. The two new fields are added at the *bottom* of the form in the Form view. To move them to the desired place, it is first necessary to insert a blank line for each one to make room for the move. Press **F9** to go to the Form screen.

   a. Move the cursor to the Reg Hours field name and use **Edit/Insert Line** to move all of the fields down 1 line.

   b. Move the cursor to the newly added field name "Emp.No." at the bottom of the form and press **F3.**

   c. Move the cursor to the blank line you just inserted and press **Enter.**

   d. Repeat those steps to move the Dept field right under the Emp.No. field.

   e. For both new fields, use **Format/Field Size** and make the width = 10 and the height = 1.

6. Still in the Form view, move the cursor just *below* the last field name, "Gross Pay," and add another new field name called "Remarks." Make the width = 15 and the heigth = 3.

7. Now move the cursor eight spaces to the right of the Name field and on that same line, add the following *label*:

Departments

Production
Office
Sales

8. Now move to the new field, "Dept," in record 1 of the Form screen. Since most employees are in the Sales department, we cause that field to automatically insert *Sales* for each record. Then, if someone works in another department, you can type that department name over *Sales*.

   a. In the Dept field content area type =**"Sales** and press **Enter**.

   b. "Sales" is immediately placed in that field in *all* of the records.

9. Starting with record number 1 in the List view, update the records by entering the following in the Emp.No. field:

	Emp.No.
Joe Smith	**13**
Mary Johnson	**6**
Gayle McCrary	**10**

10. In the List view enter the data for the following three new records. To get back to the Name field after completing a record, press the **Down Arrow** key to move into the next record and then press the **Home** key.

Name	Emp.No	Dept	Reg Hrs	O/T Hours	Pay Rate	Gross Pay
Bob Newton	11	Sales	40	4.5	8.00	374.00
Jan Estes	4	Office	40	0	4.25	170.00
Ben Baker	2	Sales	32	0	4.25	136.00

11. Go to the Form view and type these "remarks" in that field for the following two employees. Notice as you type, the text moves to the next line if it does not fit on the current line.

   for Joe Smith: **due commission at the end of the month**
   for Bob Newton: **the leading salesperson for the week**

12. Save the database.

13. Get a two-page printout while in the Form view using **Print/Print**.

   a. Remove the "X" in the "Page breaks between records" bracket.

   b. Type **.5** in the brackets for "Space between records."

   c. Under "Print which records:," select *all records*.

   d. Under "Print which items:," select *all items*.

14. Compare your results of the printouts with the key on the next two pages.

```
╔══════════════════════════════════════════════╗
║ ┌────────────────────────────────────────────┐ ║
║ │              KEY: DRILL-11                   │ ║
║ │          Chapter 4 - Section 3               │ ║
║ └────────────────────────────────────────────┘ ║
╚══════════════════════════════════════════════╝
```

```
      Weekly Payroll
--------------------------
Name: Joe Smith                        Departments
Emp.No.:          13                   -----------
Dept: Sales                            Production
Reg Hours:        40                   Office
O/T Hours:        3.5                  Sales
Pay Rate:       $7.50
Gross Pay:     $339.38
Remarks: due commission
         at the end of
         the month


      Weekly Payroll
--------------------------
Name: Mary Johnson                     Departments
Emp.No.:           6                   -----------
Dept: Sales                            Production
Reg Hours:        35                   Office
O/T Hours:         0                   Sales
Pay Rate:       $3.90
Gross Pay:     $136.50
Remarks:


      Weekly Payroll
--------------------------
Name: Gayle McCrary                    Departments
Emp.No.:          10                   -----------
Dept: Sales                            Production
Reg Hours:        40                   Office
O/T Hours:         2                   Sales
Pay Rate:       $5.75
Gross Pay:     $247.25
Remarks:
```

```
        Weekly Payroll
----------------------------
Name: Bob Newton                Departments
Emp.No.:            11          ------------
Dept: Sales                     Production
Reg Hours:          40          Office
O/T Hours:          4.5         Sales
Pay Rate:       $8.00
Gross Pay:      $374.00
Remarks: the leading
         salesperson for
         the week


        Weekly Payroll
----------------------------
Name: Jan Estes                 Departments
Emp.No.:            4           ------------
Dept: Office                    Production
Reg Hours:          40          Office
O/T Hours:          0           Sales
Pay Rate:       $4.25
Gross Pay:      $170.00
Remarks:


        Weekly Payroll
----------------------------
Name: Ben Baker                 Departments
Emp.No.:            2           ------------
Dept: Office                    Production
Reg Hours:          32          Office
O/T Hours:          0           Sales
Pay Rate:       $4.25
Gross Pay:      $136.00
Remarks:
```

DRILL-12

Tasks This drill lets you practice the following:

- Formatting in List view
- Hiding and redisplaying fields
- Locking and unlocking protected fields
- Delete a field and a record
- Setting vertical and horizontal page breaks and print

Procedure From the information below, complete the steps for DRILL-12.

If you have any problems, review the material in Chapter 4, Sections 2 and 3.

1. Open the file REUNION.WDB from your disk.

2. Move the cursor to the City field. Use **Format/Style** and in the "alignment" box turn on **Right** and in the "styles" box turn on **bold** and press **Enter**.

3. Move the cursor to the Status field. Use **Format/Field Width** and change the width to zero (**0**) and press **Enter**. The field should have disappeared.

4. Now you "insert page breaks" so you can print just the first 3 fields for the first 10 records.

   a. Move the cursor to the Age field and use **Print/Insert Page Break**. Choose **field** and press **Enter**.

   b. Move the cursor to the field name "Last" and go down to the eleventh record (Baker). Use **Print/Insert Page Break**, choose **record,** and press **Enter**.

   c. Use **Print/Print,** turn on **Print specific pages**, specify page number 1 for "Pages," and press **Enter**.

This should give you a printout of just the first 3 fields for the first 10 records. Notice the *City* column is in bold and aligned to the right as previously formatted.

5. Move the cursor to the top of the City field in the List view. Use **Select/Field** to highlight the entire field. Use the Edit Menu to choose **Delete Record/Field,** and the entire field is deleted.

6. Choose **Select/Go To** and in the Go to box, type **Status** and press **Enter**. Now, choose **Format/Field Width** and type **7** as the field width and press **Enter**. The Status field that was hidden in step 3 should reappear.

7. All of the fields were locked initially. Go to the Age field and choose **Select/Field** to highlight that entire field. Now use **Format/Style** to remove the "X" by *locked* and press **Enter**. Next, use **Options/Protect Data** to protect the data in all of the fields that are still locked (all of them but the Age field). Go to any field and try to enter something. You will find the only field that allows a change is the Age field.

8. Do *not* save these changes; they were just used for these explanations.

9. Compare your printout to the key on the following page.

KEY: DRILL-12
Chapter 4 - Section 3

Smith	Aaron	Austin
Smith	Fred	San Antonio
Scott	Becky	Houston
Spiller	Cynthia	Fort Worth
White	James	El Paso
Stephenson	Don	San Antonio
Stevenson	Robert	Houston
Smith	William	Lake Jackson
Mancuso	Debbie	Freeport
Smith	Valerie	Galveston

SECTION 4

Skills to be learned in this section

- Querying the database
- Entering a criterion
- Troubleshooting queries

QUERYING THE DATABASE

This lets you display all the records that match certain criteria. The Query screen resembles the Form screen and provides the framework for a query. Each field can contain one rule, called a criterion, that is used to determine which database records to display or hide.

If the fields in a record match *every* criterion, the record is displayed on the List screen when you exit the Query screen by pressing F10. If even one of the criteria doesn't match, it hides the record.

Before you apply another set of criteria to the Query, be sure to remove the criteria from the last query. Choose the Edit/Delete Query commands and it removes all criteria previously selected.

ENTERING A CRITERION

A criterion is entered from the Query screen. You select the field into which you want to enter the criterion and then when you return to the List screen, the records that satisfied the query are listed. All the other records that did not satisfy the query are hidden. Some criterion examples are:

In the **Price** field, **>15&<25**...finds all prices greater than 15 and less than 25

In the **Last Name** field, **="Smith"**..displays all last names of SMITH

Examples of Queries

Operator	Name	Example	Records It Would Find
=	Equals	=30	the number 30
		="TX"	tx (or) TX (or) Tx
<	Less than	<20	values less than 20
		<"N"	data alphabetically before "N"
>	Greater than	>25	values greater than 25
		>"Nathan"	data alphabetically after "Nathan"
<=	Less than or equal to	<=50	finds values that are 50 and less than 50
>=	Greater than or equal to	>=50	finds values that are 50 and greater than 50
		>="u"	finds anything that begins with "u,v,w, x,y, or z"
<>	Not equal to	<>50	finds all values except 50
|	Or	==10|=20	finds only the values 10 or 20
&	And	>20&<80	finds the values between 20 and 80

TROUBLESHOOTING QUERIES

If you receive an ERROR message or "Invalid reference" or "Wrong operand type," check your query against the following:

** If the query contains text, did you remember to put quotation marks (") before and after the text?

    Incorrect: <>tx

    Correct: **<>"tx"**

** If the query contains a date, is it enclosed in single quotes?

    Incorrect: >=1/1/90

    Correct: **>='1/1/90'**

** If the query is searching for a number that was entered as text (such a zip code), did you remember to enclose it in quotes?

    Incorrect: =77566

    Correct: **="77566"**

** Did you put in too many or too few operators?

    Incorrect: ="Mary"|"Janet"

    Correct: **="Mary"|="Janet"**

** Did you close the quotes around a text entry?

    Incorrect: =="TX|=CA

    Correct: **=="TX"|="CA"**

** Did you use the AND operator when you should have used the OR operator, or vice versa?

    <>"TX"|<>"CA" finds **all** of the states in your database

    <>"TX"&<>"CA" finds **all** of the states **except** TX and CA

Note: If you receive one of the error messages, press Enter to clear the message from the screen. Check the Message Line at the bottom of the screen to see if you are in the *Edit Mode*. If you are not, press the F2 key so that you can edit your query.

Also, check the following:

** Is the *field name* spelled correctly?

** Did you delete the previous query before entering the new one?

** Did you enter the criteria in the correct field?

DRILL-13

Tasks This drill lets you practice the following:

- Using "search" and "goto" commands
- Hiding and switching records
- Sorting and querying the database
- Printing a database

Procedure From the information below, complete the steps for DRILL-13.

If you have any problems, review the material in Chapter 4, Sections 3 and 4.

1. Open the file REUNION.WDB from your disk.

2. Go to the List screen and press **Ctrl+Home**. Use **Select/Go To**, type **23** in the Go to: box, and press **Enter**. The cursor should have moved to record number 23.

3. Press **Ctrl+Home** again. This time use **Select/Search**, type **Houston**, and press **Enter**. The cursor should have moved to the *City field* of record number 3. Press **F7** to repeat the search and count how many times it finds Houston in the 25 records (it should have stopped a total of six times).

4. Use **View/Query** to go to the Query screen and enter the queries below. To return to the List screen to see which records satisfied the criteria entered, you can choose **View/List** or just press **F10** as the shortcut key.

Remember when you return to the Query screen to choose **Edit/Delete Query** to remove the previous criteria before entering the new criteria.

Apply the following queries (press **Enter** after you type them) and write on the line provided how many records satisfied each query:

	QUERY	FIELD FOR QUERY
____	=50	AGE
____	="San Antonio"	City
____	<"Stevenson"	Last
____	>="m"	Last
____	=="Dallas"|="Fort Worth"	City

5. Apply the following queries and write on the lines provided how many records satisfied each query:

____ All *males over 30* that *earn at least $35,000*

____ All *single females* that *live in Houston*

____ All that are *older than 25 and younger than 40*

____ All *married men* that *live in Dallas*

6. Use **Select/Switch Hidden Records**. This hides the list for married men that live in Dallas and shows all of the others.

7. Choose **Select/Show All Records** to restore any hidden records. Use **Select/Sort Records** and set the sort fields as shown below. Then perform the following sorts and get a printout after each.

   a. Sort the *First Field* on "age" (descending) and the *Second Field* on "income" (descending). Use **Print/Headers & Footers** and type **&l7a)** in the header box before you get the printout.

   b. Sort the *First Field* on "city" (ascending) and the *Second Field* on "age" (ascending). Use **Print/Headers & Footers** and change the header to **&l7b)** before you get the printout.

8. Compare your printouts to the keys on the following pages.

9. Close the database without saving.

```
╔══════════════════════════════════════════════════╗
║                 KEY: DRILL-13                      ║
║              Chapter 4 - Section 4                 ║
╚══════════════════════════════════════════════════╝
```

4. Answers

	QUERY	FIELD FOR QUERY
1	=50	AGE
4	="San Antonio"	City
21	<"Stevenson"	Last
12	>="m"	Last
7	=="Dallas"|="Fort Worth"	City

5. Answers

8	All males over 30 that earn at least $35,000
2	All single females that live in Houston
12	All that are older than 25 and younger than 40
1	All married men that live in Dallas

---- **FIRST PRINTOUT** ----

7 a)

Baker	Allan	Dallas	60	$25,000	2	m
Stephenson	Don	San Antonio	51	$105,000	1	m
Sutton	Sam	Dallas	50	$48,000	1	m
Eaton	Sam	Dallas	46	$78,000	2	m
Sullivan	Beth	San Antonio	45	$67,000	2	f
Smith	Aaron	Austin	42	$45,500	1	m
Duncan	Douglas	Fort Worth	41	$93,500	2	m
Smith	Fred	San Antonio	40	$60,000	2	m
Gibson	Marie	Dallas	39	$43,000	1	f
Jordan	Joyce	Houston	37	$55,000	2	f
White	James	El Paso	37	$29,000	1	m
Stevenson	Robert	Houston	34	$49,000	2	m
Scott	Becky	Houston	33	$37,500	2	f
Finch	Norman	Houston	33	$35,000	1	m
Hernandez	Johnny	Houston	33	$31,500	2	m
Anderson	Jim	Houston	30	$41,500	2	m
Johnson	Betty	Lubbock	30	$34,500	2	f
Carter	Carolyn	Fort Worth	29	$42,000	1	f
Higgins	Regina	Texarkana	27	$32,500	1	f
Smith	William	Lake Jackson	26	$32,000	1	m
Flynn	Frances	Lake Jackson	25	$25,000	1	f
Glover	Sue	San Antonio	25	$18,900	2	f
Spiller	Cynthia	Fort Worth	24	$24,000	2	f
Smith	Valerie	Galveston	24	$10,500	2	f
Mancuso	Debbie	Freeport	22	$17,000	1	f

---- SECOND PRINTOUT ----

7 b)

Smith	Aaron	Austin	42	$45,500	1	m
Gibson	Marie	Dallas	39	$43,000	1	f
Eaton	Sam	Dallas	46	$78,000	2	m
Sutton	Sam	Dallas	50	$48,000	1	m
Baker	Allan	Dallas	60	$25,000	2	m
White	James	El Paso	37	$29,000	1	m
Spiller	Cynthia	Fort Worth	24	$24,000	2	f
Carter	Carolyn	Fort Worth	29	$42,000	1	f
Duncan	Douglas	Fort Worth	41	$93,500	2	m
Mancuso	Debbie	Freeport	22	$17,000	1	f
Smith	Valerie	Galveston	24	$10,500	2	f
Anderson	Jim	Houston	30	$41,500	2	m
Scott	Becky	Houston	33	$37,500	2	f
Finch	Norman	Houston	33	$35,000	1	m
Hernandez	Johnny	Houston	33	$31,500	2	m
Stevenson	Robert	Houston	34	$49,000	2	m
Jordan	Joyce	Houston	37	$55,000	2	f
Flynn	Frances	Lake Jackson	25	$25,000	1	f
Smith	William	Lake Jackson	26	$32,000	1	m
Johnson	Betty	Lubbock	30	$34,500	2	f
Glover	Sue	San Antonio	25	$18,900	2	f
Smith	Fred	San Antonio	40	$60,000	2	m
Sullivan	Beth	San Antonio	45	$67,000	2	f
Stephenson	Don	San Antonio	51	$105,000	1	m
Higgins	Regina	Texarkana	27	$32,500	1	f

Chapter 5

INTEGRATED
PROCEDURES

"Integrated" software means that the menu commands and procedures are similar, that the files can easily be shared between applications, and that all of the main computer applications are contained in one package.

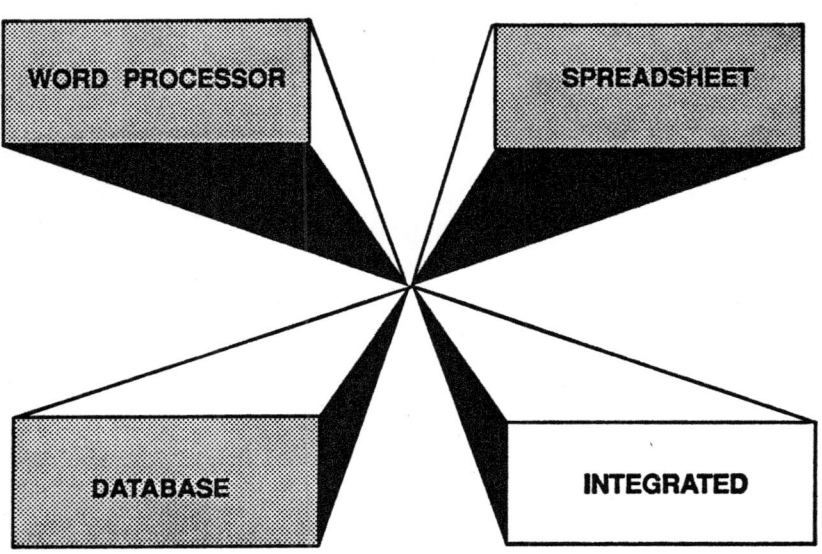

Skills to be learned in this chapter

- Copying data from the Word Processor to the Database
- Copying data from the Word Processor to the Spreadsheet
- Merging a chart into a Word Processor file
- Sizing a merged chart in a Word Processor file
- Copying data from the Database to the Word Processor
- Copying data from the Spreadsheet to the Word Processor
- Copying data between the Database and the Spreadsheet
- Creating and printing form letters with the Database

WORKS makes it easy to get information from one tool to another and to integrate results from the different tools for analysis or presentation.

You use the Move command to move information *within* a file, but *not between* different WORKS tools. You use the Copy command for exchanging between tools.

COPYING FROM THE WORD PROCESSOR TO THE DATABASE OR SPREADSHEET

To copy information from a word processor file to a database or spreadsheet file, it must be organized in rows and columns, with tabs and paragraph marks. If the text is not organized this way, you need to edit it so that tab marks replace spaces, commas, or other characters that separate the information. Make sure that each line ends with a paragraph mark or a down arrow. The Shift+Enter keystrokes cause the down arrow marker. The data that ends with a down arrow marker or paragraph marker is placed in separate cells; the other is placed in the same cell.

1. Make sure that both the word processor file and the spreadsheet or database file are open. If you are copying to a database file, make sure you are in the List screen.

2. Activate the word processor file and select the data you want to copy using the F8 key.

3. From the Edit Menu, choose Copy.

4. Using the Window Menu, switch to the spreadsheet or the database file into which you want the information copied.

5. In the spreadsheet or database file, move the cursor to the place you want the word processor information copied, and press Enter.

Note: WORKS does *not* transfer the character formats from the word processor to the spreadsheet or database file. If you don't want to lose the current cell or field values in the spreadsheet or database, be sure to insert the copied information at the bottom of the database or spreadsheet, or leave enough empty cells to accommodate the incoming data.

MERGING A CHART INTO A WORD PROCESSOR FILE

A chart created using the spreadsheet can be merged into a word processor file. The word processor file can then be printed with the chart in it. You can adjust the size of the chart to the size desired and place it on the page vertically (Portrait orientation) or sideways on the page (horizontally is the Landscape orientation).

Before inserting, make sure that the spreadsheet file with the chart you want and the word processor file you want to insert the chart into are both open.

1. Open the spreadsheet that has the chart attached to it that you want inserted in the word processor file.

2. Open the word processor file into which you want the chart inserted.

3. In the word processor file, move the cursor to where you want to insert the chart.

4. From the Edit Menu, choose the Insert Chart command. In the Insert Chart box, the Spreadsheets list box shows the files that are open. The Charts list box shows the charts available for the spreadsheet you selected.

5. In the Spreadsheets list box, bring the *selection bar* down to select the spreadsheet that has the chart you want merged into the word processor file.

6. Move to the Charts list box and bring the *selection bar* down to select the chart you want.

7. Press Enter and WORKS inserts a chart placeholder that looks like this:

chart SHEET1.WKS:CHART1

SHEET1.WKS is the name of the *spreadsheet*; **CHART1** is the name of the *chart*.

Note: You can use the F8 key to select the chart placeholder and move it around as needed using the Move command in the Edit Menu. Or you could copy it to some other location. To substitute the chart you have inserted, select the chart placeholder message and delete it. Then follow the procedures to insert a chart.

SIZING A CHART IN A WORD PROCESSOR FILE

When you have the chart where you want it, you can adjust its size to fit your word processor file.

1. Make the word processor file with the chart placeholder in it the active file.

2. Move the cursor to the chart placeholder.

3. From the Format Menu, choose Indents & Spacing. A chart dialog box is displayed with some options that are the same as those in the paragraph dialog box. The options for "Chart height" and "Orientation" apply only to charts.

4. In the Left indent and Right indent text boxes, type measurements (in inches) to determine how far in from the current margins you want the chart. These settings determine the *width* and *placement* of the chart. When WORKS prints your file, it sizes the chart to fit the space defined by the measurements in the Left indent, Right indent, and Chart Height text boxes.

5. In the Chart Height text box, type the vertical size in inches. The height refers to the *length* of the X-axis.

6. In the Space before and Space after text boxes, type the number of lines you want to leave before and after the chart.

7. Under Orientation, select *Portrait* to print the chart with its bottom or X-axis parallel to the bottom of the page or *Landscape* to print the chart parallel to the left side of the page. Press Enter to record the settings.

Note: When you print a word processor file with a chart in it, WORKS has to be able to access the spreadsheet that has the chart you want to include. Both the word processor file and the spreadsheet file *must* be open.

COPYING FROM THE SPREADSHEET OR DATABASE TO THE WORD PROCESSOR

WORKS copies the spreadsheet or database values into the word processor as text. You can then edit it as you would any other text in a word processor file.

Character styles (bold, italic, underline) are preserved for the word processor, as are the paragraph alignments. The copied text takes on the font of the part of the word processor file you copied it into.

1. Activate the spreadsheet or database file and select the information you want to copy using the F8 key.

2. From the Edit Menu choose Copy.

3. Switch to the word processor file into which you want to copy the information.

4. In the word processor file, move the cursor to the position where you want to copy the information and press Enter.

COPYING INFORMATION BETWEEN THE DATABASE AND THE SPREADSHEET

When you copy information from a database to a spreadsheet, each database record becomes a spreadsheet row, and each database field becomes a spreadsheet column. The reverse is true when you copy from a spreadsheet to a database.

1. Make sure both the database file and the spreadsheet file are open.

2. In the database file make sure you are in the List screen.

3. Select the fields and records or the rows and columns you want to copy using the F8 key.

4. From the Edit Menu, choose Copy.

5. Using the Window Menu, switch to the file you want to copy the information into.

6. Move to the cell in the upper left corner of the area you want to copy the information into and press Enter.

CREATING FORM LETTERS

Form letters use a word processor file and a database file. Both must be open at the same time, with the word processor file the active file.

In the word processor file, you type the text that will remain the same for all of the form letters. As you create the form letter, you insert placeholders for the data that will be merged from the database file. To do this, you use the Insert Field command from the Edit Menu.

1. Move the cursor in the word processor file to where you want to insert a placeholder.

2. Use the Insert Field command from the Edit Menu.

3. In the database list box, select the file you want to use. WORKS displays a list of the field names for that file in the Fields list box.

4. In the Fields list box select the appropriate field name and press Enter to insert that placeholder into the word processor file.

5. Repeat steps 1 through 4 for each database field name to be inserted into the word processor file. You can format the placeholders as you would any word processor text.

6. Below is an example of a short form letter showing how the placeholders look after they have all been inserted.

Dear <<FIRST NAME>>,

The twentieth reunion is currently being planned. Please start making arrangements to have the <<LAST NAME>> family there for the weekend of October 18-20. In a few weeks you will be receiving additional information at <<ADDRESS>> that will finalize the meeting places and times. Remember to keep those dates open.

PRINTING FORM LETTERS

WORKS prints one copy of the form letter for each visible record in the database file. If you want to print form letters using some of the database records, but not all of them, you must go to the database file and use the Query command to select those you want. Remember, the database hides the other records, and hidden records are not printed.

The form letters are printed in the same order as the records are listed in the database file. If you want to print the form letters in a particular order, such as alphabetical by last name or by postal code, use the Sort command in the database file after you have hidden any not wanted.

1. Open the database file you need. If you have to query and sort the records, do so before printing.

2. Open the word processor file. Be sure the placeholders for the database field names are inserted before printing.

3. From the Print Menu, choose Print Form Letters. A "Databases:" list box is displayed.

4. If needed, move the selection bar down to select the database file you want to use and press Enter.

5. Press Enter again to activate printing. As the form letters are printed, the status line displays the total number of form letters to be printed and the number that have already been printed.

DRILL-14

Tasks This drill lets you practice the following:

- Merging a spreadsheet chart into a word processor file
- Sizing the chart to fit the file
- Printing the word processor file with the chart in it

Procedure From the information below, complete the steps for DRILL-14.

If you have any problems, review the material in the first part of this chapter.

1. Open a new word processor file and type the following. Justify it using **Ctrl-J.**

   This is going to be a demonstration of merging a chart from a spreadsheet into a word processor file. The chart will be inserted below this paragraph, sized, and its orientation checked. Then this file will be printed out with the chart in it.

Note: Press **Enter** after typing the paragraph to make room for the chart placeholder.

2. Open from your data disk a spreadsheet named MERGE_CH.WKS. The chart to merge that is attached to this spreadsheet is named 3STOOGES.

3. Use the Window Menu to make your new word processor file the active file.

4. Use the "Merging a chart in the word processor file" instructions outlined in the first part of this chapter. The chart placeholder is an asterisk (*) and you need to place the cursor on the placeholder to make changes using the Format Menu.

   For the chart we want these settings from the **Format/Indents & Spacing**:

Left indent:	**.5"**
Right indent:	**.5"**
Space before:	**2 lines**
Space after:	**1 lines**
Chart height:	**4.5"**
Orientation:	**Portrait**

5. Now type the following text *below* the chart placeholder:

   Now some more text is typed after the chart was inserted into this file.

6. Save the file as MERGE_CH.WPS and print it out.

7. Compare your printout to the key on the following page.

KEY: DRILL 14

This is going to be a demonstration of merging a chart from a spreadsheet into a word processor file. The chart will be inserted below this paragraph, sized, and its orientation checked. Then this file will be printed out with the chart in it.

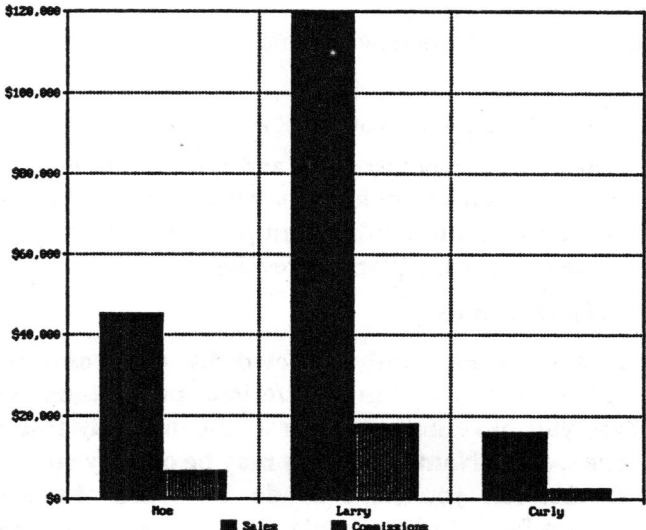

Now some text is typed after the chart was inserted into this file.

113

DRILL-15

Tasks This drill lets you practice the following:

- Creating a form letter in the word processor
- Inserting database field name placeholders in the letter
- Merging and printing form letters using a database file

Procedure From the information below, complete the steps for DRILL-15.

If you have any problems, review the material in the first part of this chapter.

1. Open the database file on your disk named ADDRESS1.WDB.

2. Open a new word processor file and type in the letter below. When you get to a placeholder, do *not* type it in, use **Insert Field** from the Edit Menu to let the word processor insert it for you. Refer to the steps in Chapter 5 to review the process.

    Dear <<First Name>>:

    You have been randomly selected by our computers to participate in a once in a lifetime promotion. <<First Name>>, you have nothing to lose and possibly millions to gain. The <<Last Name>> family may be on easy street in the near future. All you have to do is return the enclosed subscription form to be eligible. Then the mailman may be stopping at <<Street>> in <<City>> to deliver your prizes.

    Yours truly,

    The Briber Subscriber Co.

3. Use **Print Form Letters** from the Print Menu to get a printout for each record in the database.

4. Compare your printouts to the keys on the following pages.

KEY #1: DRILL 15

Dear Mary:

You have been randomly selected by our computers to participate in a once in a lifetime promotion. Mary, you have nothing to lose and possibly millions to gain. The Jones family may be on easy street in the near future. All you have to do is return the enclosed subscription form to be eligible. Then the mailman may be stopping at 123 Any Street in New Orleans to deliver your prizes.

Yours truly,

The Briber Subscriber Co.

KEY #2: DRILL 15

Dear Fred:

You have been randomly selected by our computers to participate in a once in a lifetime promotion. Fred, you have nothing to lose and possibly millions to gain. The Flintstone family may be on easy street in the near future. All you have to do is return the enclosed subscription form to be eligible. Then the mailman may be stopping at 404 Rock Lane in Boulder to deliver your prizes.

Yours truly,

The Briber Subscriber Co.

KEY #3: DRILL 15

Dear Clark:

You have been randomly selected by our computers to participate in a once in a lifetime promotion. Clark, you have nothing to lose and possibly millions to gain. The Kent family may be on easy street in the near future. All you have to do is return the enclosed subscription form to be eligible. Then the mailman may be stopping at 999 Airmale Drive in Metropolis to deliver your prizes.

Yours truly,

The Briber Subscriber Co.

Chapter 6
COMMUNICATIONS

Since a modem is necessary to effectively demonstrate how a communications package operates, this chapter is only intended to provide an overview of some of the capabilities available.

With the communications tool in WORKS, you can exchange information with other computers in the same room, across town, or across the country.

You can scan current stock prices, book airline flights, check your bank balance, read computer bulletin boards, play games against an unknown foe, search an encyclopedia database, etc.

To get started in the use of communications, you need a modem and a telephone line or a cable that connects your computer directly to another computer, called the host computer.

MODEM

Modem is short for MOdulator/DEModulator. It is a device that enables your computer to communicate with a host over ordinary telephone lines.

BAUD RATE

The speed at which information can be transmitted is called the baud rate. 300 bauds is approximately 30 characters per second. A 1200-baud rate would then be about 120 (4 times the 300-baud rate).

SETTINGS

Before you can make a successful connection with the host computer, your communication package settings must be totally compatible with that of the host computer. The *terminal command* and the *communications command* in the Options Menu have most of these settings.

121

SENDING AND RECEIVING FILES

You can send text (*upload*) using the Transfer menu's Send Text command. You save text from a host computer (*download*) by using the Transfer menu's Capture Text command.

CONNECTING AND DISCONNECTING FROM THE HOST COMPUTER

To begin a communications session, you choose the Connect command from the Connect Menu. You disconnect in exactly the same way when you are ready to finish a session.

OTHER TERMS

Receive/Send protocol A *protocol* is any set of procedures two computers follow when communicating. To ensure that error-free transmission occurs, special checks can be implemented and if too many errors take place, WORKS cancels the transfer.

On-line *On-line* means connecting to and communicating with another computer.

Terminal-type computer This is when your computer is connected to a host computer and doesn't use its own computing power. It emulates the host computer's hardware.

Handshake The capability of the computers connected to send pause signals, called XON and XOFF (short for TRANSMIT ON and TRANSMIT OFF), when the data flow from one comes faster than the other can receive it.

Index

active file, 5

baud rate, 121

charts, 50
  borders, 53
  components of, 50
  formatting, 52
  gridlines, 53
  merging into a file, 106
  naming, 53
  printing, 54
  saving, 54
  sizing in a word processor
    file, 107
  speed, 51
  viewing, 53
communications, 3, 121

database, 65
  character, 67
  criterion, 94
  definition, 3
  deleting a field, 78
  deleting a record, 78
  designing, 68
  editing, 73
  entering numbers, 75
  entering text, 74
  field contents, 68
  field creation, 70-71
  field formula, 68, 75
  field name, 68
  formatting numbers, 72
  formula bar, 74
  go to command, 82
  hiding fields, 85
  hiding records, 85
  inserting page breaks, 86
  inserting rows and
    columns, 76
  labels, 68
  locking cells, 83
  moving a field, 77
  printing, 76
  proposing a field's
    contents, 83
  query, 68, 94-96
  record, 68
  search command, 82
  sorting records, 84
dialog boxes, 6
directory, 5

file extension, 4
file names, 4
file, 4
  create, 5, 11
  new, 11
  open, 5, 11
  printing, 13
  save, 6
form letters, 109-110
formulas, 35

handshake, 122
headers and footers, 25

insert mode, 7
integrated, 3, 103

menus, 6
modem, 121
mouse, 7

opening an existing file, 11

printing, 13, 35, 54, 76, 110

"save as" command, 13

Other Books from Wordware Publishing, Inc.

Business-Professional Books
Business Emotions
The Business Side of Writing
Confessions of a Banker
Hawks Do, Buzzards Don't
How to Win Pageants
Innovation, Inc.
Investor Beware
MegaTraits
Occupying the Summit
Steps to Strategic Management
To Be or Not to Be an S.O.B

Computer Aided Drafting
Illustrated AutoCAD (Release 10)
Illustrated AutoCAD (Release 11)
Illustrated AutoCAD for the Mac
Illustrated AutoLISP
Illustrated AutoSketch 1.04
Illustrated AutoSketch 2.0
Illustrated GenericCADD Level 3

Database Management
The DataFlex Developer's Handbook
Illustrated dBASE III Plus
Illustrated dBASE IV 1.1
Illustrated FoxPro
Illustrated FoxPro 2.0
Illustrated Paradox 3.0 Volume II (2nd Ed.)

Desktop Publishing
Achieving Graphic Impact with Ventura 2.0
Desktop Publisher's Dictionary
Illustrated PFS:First Publisher 2.0
Illustrated PFS:First Publisher 2.0 & 3.0
Illustrated PageMaker 3.0
Illustrated PageMaker 4.0
Illustrated Ready, Set, Go! 4.5 (Macintosh)
Illustrated Ventura 2.0
Illustrated Ventura 3.0 (Windows Ed.)
Illustrated Ventura 3.0 (DOS/GEM Ed.)
The Desktop Studio: Multimedia with the Amiga
Ventura Troubleshooting Guide

General and Advanced Topics
Illustrated DacEasy Accounting 4.1
Illustrated Harvard Graphics 2.3
Illustrated Novell NetWare 2.15 (2nd Ed.)
Illustrated Novell NetWare 3.1.1
Novell NetWare: Adv. Tech. and Applications
Understanding 3COM Networks

Integrated
Illustrated Enable/OA
Illustrated Framework III
Illustrated Microsoft Works 2.0
Illustrated Q & A 3.0 (2nd Ed.)

Programming Languages
Illustrated C Programming (ANSI) (2nd Ed.)
Illustrated Clipper 5.0 (2nd Ed.)
Illustrated QBasic for MS-DOS 5.00
The DataFlex Developer's Handbook
The FOCUS Developer's Handbook
Graphic Programming with Turbo Pascal
GUI Programming with C

Programming Languages (cont.)
Illustrated Turbo C++
Illustrated Turbo Debugger and Tools
Illustrated Turbo Pascal 5.5
Illustrated Turbo Pascal 6.0

Spreadsheet
Illustrated Lotus 1-2-3 2.01
Illustrated Lotus 1-2-3 Rel. 3.0
Illustrated Lotus 1-2-3 Rel. 2.2
Illustrated Microsoft Excel 2.10 (IBM)
Illustrated Microsoft Excel 1.5 (Macintosh)
Illustrated Quattro
Illustrated SuperCalc 5

Systems and Operating Guides
Illustrated Microsoft Windows 2.0
Illustrated Microsoft Windows 3.0
Illustrated MS/PC DOS 3.3
Illustrated MS/PC DOS 4.0 (6th Ed.)
Illustrated MS DOS 5.0
Illustrated UNIX System V

Word Processing
Illustrated DisplayWrite 4
Illustrated Microsoft Word 5.0 (PC)
Illustrated WordPerfect 1.0 (Macintosh)
Illustrated WordPerfect 5.0
Illustrated WordPerfect 5.1
Illustrated WordPerfect for Windows
Illustrated WordStar 6.0
Illustrated WordStar Professional (Rel. 5)
WordPerfect: Advanced Applications Handbook
WordPerfect Wizardry Adv. Tech. and Applications

Popular Applications Series
Cost Control Using Lotus 1-2-3
Creating Newsletters with Ventura
Desktop Publishing with WordPerfect
Learn CorelDRAW! in a Day
Learn DOS in a Day
Learn Lotus 1-2-3 in a Day
Learn Microsoft Works in a Day
Learn PAL in a Day
Learn Paradox in a Day
Learn PlanPerfect in a Day
Learn Quattro Pro in a Day
Learn WordPerfect in a Day
Mailing Lists using dBASE
Object-Oriented Programming using Turbo C++
Presentations with Harvard Graphics
WordPerfect Macros

Regional
Exploring the Alamo Legends
Forget the Alamo
The Great Texas Airship Mystery
100 Days in Texas: The Alamo Letters
Rainy Days in Texas Funbook
Texas Highway Humor
Texas Wit and Wisdom
That Cat Won't Flush
They Don't Have to Die
This Dog'll Hunt
Unsolved Texas Mysteries

Call Wordware Publishing, Inc. for names of the bookstores in your area
(214) 423-0090